The Coach Roads to Brighton

Geoffrey Hewlett

Pen Press

© Geoffrey Hewlett 2014

All rights reserved

No part of this publication may be reproduced, stored in a retrieval system, or transmitted in any form or by any means, without the prior permission in writing of the publisher, nor be otherwise circulated in any form of binding or cover other than that in which it is published and without a similar condition including this condition being imposed on the subsequent purchaser.

First published in Great Britain

All paper used in the printing of this book has been made from wood grown in managed, sustainable forests.

ISBN13: 978-1-78003-775-2

Printed and bound in the UK
Pen Press is an imprint of
Author Essentials
4 The Courtyard
Falmer BN1 9PQ

A catalogue record of this book is available from the British Library

Cover design by Jacqueline Abromeit

To the coachmen who followed the roads to Brighton, and to my wife Elizabeth who has encouraged and helped me while following their tracks.

Contents

Chapter 1   1
The Brighton Roads

Chapter 2   18
The Lewes Route: London to Streatham

Chapter 3   39
The Lewes route: Streatham to Godstone

Chapter 4   57
The Lewes route: Godstone to Lewes

Chapter 5   75
The Lewes route: Wych Cross to Brighton through Chailey

Chapter 6   95
The Horsham route: Kennington to Dorking

Chapter 7   115
The Horsham route: Dorking to Brighton

Chapter 8   143
The "Classic" Route: London to Crawley

Chapter 9   170
The "Classic" Route: Crawley to Brighton

Chapter 10   193
New roads for the "Golden Age"

Chapter 11   211
The Alternative Routes and the End of the Coaching Age

The Coach Roads from London to Brighton

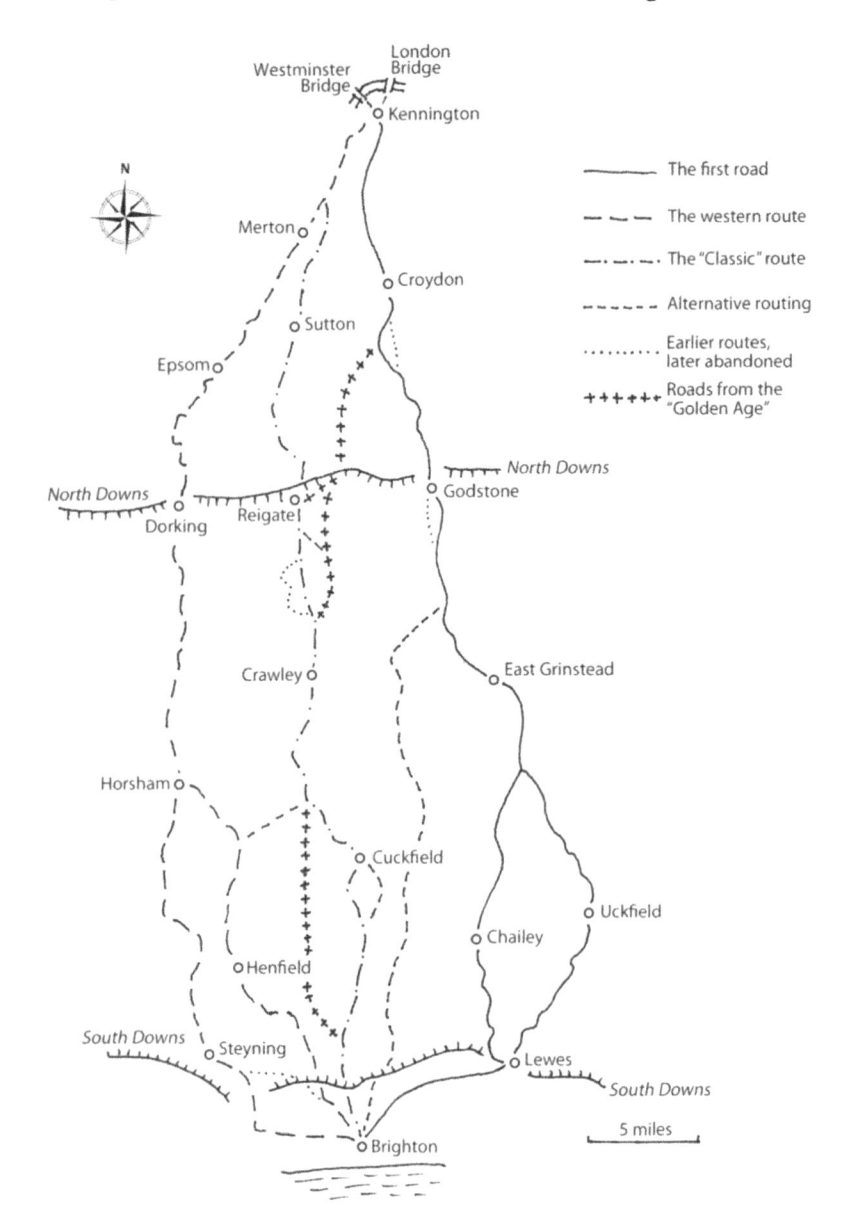

Chapter 1
The Brighton Roads

Many roads link London to the south coast. Large parts of them still follow routes which became well established in the days when travel by horse-drawn coaches was the fastest and most efficient form of transport. The coach roads to Brighton became important highways and on many miles of these the modern traveller can still enjoy the same views the coach traveller would have seen, and even refresh himself at the same coaching inns that his forebears would have used when changing their horses. One experience to be had on the roads, however, is very different today. The motorist, enclosed in his comfortable capsule, looks at the landscape through the insulating barrier of a glass window. The coach traveller was far more aware, sometimes to his extreme discomfort, of every variation in the countryside around him. He could see how the landscape dictated the line of the road. He experienced the problems of crossing valleys, climbing and descending steep hills and being exposed to the weather. He knew very well, as we tend to forget today, that the position of the roads is determined by the varied nature of the land over which they pass. The different roads, which are each known locally as 'the Brighton road', cannot be properly understood without some understanding of the land beneath them.

The distance between London and Brighton is little more than 50 miles and yet the landscape between the two is some of the most varied in Britain. Clay vales are separated by ridges of chalk and sandstone. Further variety is added by the river valleys of the Mole, the Adur and the Ouse and a small part of the headwaters of the Medway. Despite the ever-advancing tentacles of London creeping down from the north, there is much lovely countryside which has remained relatively unchanged over the centuries. George Meredith, who lived near one of the Brighton roads at Flint Cottage below Box Hill, wrote of Surrey in 1882: "Nowhere in England is richer foliage, or wilder downs and fresher woodlands." The same could be truly said today; a statement which would surely come as a surprise to many who think of the county as an urbanised appendage to London suburbia. Surrey's precious heathlands are a wild, almost primaeval landscape and the county's woodlands cover a larger percentage of the area than is found in any other English county.

Further south lies Sussex, between Surrey and the sea, epitomising the beauty and contrasts of this lovely part of England. The sandy heaths of Ashdown Forest lie above the clay of the low Weald and further south still lies the splendid escarpment of the South Downs, where the chalk ridge with its grassy slopes rises to over two hundred metres. Although modest in height compared to many of Britain's hills, the airy downland summits give unimpeded views across the Weald to the North Downs some 30 miles away. From the same viewpoints, but looking south, the gentle chalkland hills and vales gradually decline in height until they meet the sea.

Nowadays, this tract of country delights our eyes whenever we head south for a day at the seaside. How much more keenly it would have been seen by our ancestors sitting in, or on, one of the many stage coaches travelling from London to Brighton! Coach travel was not a particularly comfortable experience, especially off the major roads, but the passengers' close proximity to the landscape around them afforded them an advantage over the modern car driver, who scarcely has any time to observe the countryside he is passing through.

It would have been very clear to the Brighton coach traveller – as it still is to those who have the wit to leave their cars in favour of walking, riding or cycling through the land – that the rocks beneath their feet are the dominant reason for the changing landscape. The areas of sand, chalk and clay are strikingly distinct from each other. The rocks have determined the extent to which natural forces of erosion have shaped the land. The rocks have also provided materials with which many of the buildings and, in the past, the road surface itself, have been constructed. The road surface was, of course, a prime concern before the advent of modern hard-topped roads.

A coach leaving London to journey south was first crossing an area of gravels, sands and clays; low-lying land that gradually rose up to sandy hills. It was a land with large tracts of woodland and dry heathland, reminders of which are encountered in existing place names such as Norwood, the great forested area to the north of Croydon, and Thornton Heath, one of the many heathy areas, formerly of wide extent. This old landscape was a patchwork of good farmland set amongst the woods and heaths. Through it the roads climbed the long and gently undulating slope that culminated in the crest of the North Downs. Throughout the coaching age these roads carried increasing amounts of traffic. Their success was a major influence on the transformation from tranquil rural setting to the urbanised region it has now become.

On reaching the North Downs the roads met the chalk. In places this meant wide-open sheep walks on the short downland turf. Here, around the chalk hills of Banstead Downs, and even more extensively, Epsom Downs, some of the land has escaped excessive building and, where scrub and trees have not obliterated the grasslands, the views the coach travellers would have seen can still be enjoyed. At the southern edge of the Downs, the coaches met the most startling view they would experience on their journey from London. Reigate Hill is much more wooded now than in coaching's heyday, but to coach passengers the steep hill was a disturbing, even frightening sight and many felt a sense of relief once the precarious descent had been accomplished.

Once off the Downs the well-drained chalk is replaced by clay where the roads crossed a narrow vale, prosperous with rich towns and rich soil, after which it was back to sandy roads. These were dusty in summer, like those nearer London, but were different in their steeper ups and downs.

The clay lands to the south were then, as they are today, a totally different type of landscape compared to the regions to the north. Most modern drivers think little of this change, though many are aware that the land is flatter and there are many fields and woodlands. For the coachman, guiding his lumbering vehicle behind a team of sweating horses, the smaller details of the landscape were his primary concern. Before engineers like John Macadam showed how it was possible to construct a firm surface over the clay, the roads could become seriously rutted, and in wet weather, the clay became a saturated morass through which a heavy coach could only move with difficulty. The soft clay lands also presented another problem, that being the presence of small, steep-sided valleys, known as ghylls. Away from the road these valleys are often a feature of field boundaries and their nature as an obstacle to movement across the country is very clear. Small streams have cut into the clay and now lie incised up to ten feet or more below the level of the adjacent fields, and the places where roads crossed them were only gradually improved by the construction of high bridges. Because of these problems the most low-lying of the clay areas were avoided wherever possible and roads followed the watersheds between the main river basins.

Coach travellers, at their relatively gentle pace through the countryside, were easily able to discern the changes in the human landscape also. The fields, farms and villages had been carved out from the ancient Wealden forest, the Andredsweald of the Saxons. The blanket of forest has been eaten away over many centuries, leaving only a tattered remnant spread over the land. The result is a network of small fields, separated by wide hedgerows and the sinuous boundaries of tree-lined ghylls. It is the type of landscape known in north-western France as *bocage*, a term commonly applied by geographers to similar landscapes in England.

The coaches that chose a more easterly route to Brighton had another high, sandy area to navigate. They had to climb out of the Low Weald for a time and pass across the sandy wastes of Ashdown Forest before descending once more to the clay. The more westerly roads remained within the clay lands.

Eventually, the most striking feature of the whole journey would come into view: the ridge of the South Downs. Even the modern motorist cannot help but be aware of the fine chalk escarpment stretching across the horizon. For the coaches this was a major obstacle, but once surmounted, the roads were firm and well drained on the chalk surface, which was often reinforced with flints. This good surface made for better travelling and so, despite the gradients involved, the older roads were always built over the chalk where possible. What an immense feeling of relief the coachmen and passengers must have felt when they finally arrived at the top of the Downs! The main hazards of the journey were now past and the roads ran gently down to the welcoming coast and the comforts that awaited them in Brighton.

There are numerous roads that can be used for a journey to Brighton from London today and they still largely approximate to the routes the coaches used. They spread out over an area stretching from Horsham in the west to Uckfield in the east. So it is not surprising that an examination of the appropriate county road atlas shows 19 Brighton roads in Surrey and a further 14 in West Sussex.

No local historian of this region can ignore their particular Brighton road, yet these roads have only existed under that name for, at most, 230 years. Only in about 1780 did the small fishing village of Brighthelmstone change its name to Brighton, although it was long before the new form of name gained wide local acceptance. Every age produces its own roads, whether they be the great Roman roads that first provided coherent lines of communication throughout the country or their modern counterpart, the motorways. The Industrial Revolution and Georgian England made their own contributions, of which the roads to Brighton are but a small part.

After Roman times many roads were mainly just local affairs, linking larger places almost fortuitously. Nevertheless, great roads did gradually evolve: the Great North Road, the Dover Road, and many others which grew or declined in importance over the centuries according to the changing fortunes of the places to which they led.

The Brighton road is probably the most recently evolved of all the 'old' roads, and yet it is also one of the best known. Some books have been entirely devoted to it, and many more have references to it, from the 'road books' of coaching days to newspapers and local history publications.

In 1750 Dr Richard Russell of Lewes published a paper entitled *Glandular Diseases, or a Dissertation on the Use of Sea Water in the Affections of the Glands*. It was this paper which first established Brighton as a destination for the nobility and gentry and stimulated the growing popularity of sea bathing. As with spa towns, such as Bath and Tunbridge Wells, the early visitors made their way to Brighton in the hope that the waters, in this case sea bathing, would ameliorate their various health problems. Whether the actual journey from London improved anybody's health is doubtful, particularly when the roads had become rutted or reduced to a sea of mud. However, the increasing traffic to Brighton and, above all, the patronage of no less a person than the Regent himself who, as the Prince of Wales, first visited Brighton in 1783, started a process of road improvement which has continued to the present day with the construction of the M23 motorway. As time went by Brighton saw the development of fine buildings, and the roads leading there were much improved. The town ceased to be the preserve only of those with valetudinarian habits and became an important social centre for the well-to-do; an established rival to such fine cities as

Bath and quite eclipsing the north Kent resorts of Ramsgate and Margate.

The improvement of roads for the benefit of visitors to Brighton had a considerable effect on the lives of people living near those roads. It must have been an exciting time for a sleepy countryside region where, despite the relative proximity to London, little had changed for centuries. Small villages and hamlets lived their own lives, surrounded by their own fields and woodlands. Suddenly another world burst upon them. Fine coaches were demanding service from small wayside inns and the inhabitants of remote hamlets could glimpse the sophisticated world of London society as a lord's carriage made its way past the ploughman in his roadside field.

Inns beside the Brighton road saw a great increase in trade and the trustees of turnpike trusts were given a powerful incentive to create new roads, and to improve old ones as there was now a reasonable chance of seeing a return on their investment. Gradually the whole network of Brighton roads spread out across the Surrey and Sussex Weald. Some were already important as they linked major local towns to London. Well-established places such as Reigate, East Grinstead, Sutton, Croydon, Epsom and Horsham were all beneficiaries of the increased traffic to Brighton. Other much smaller places also grew in importance. The villages of Streatham, Merton and Clapham grew in significance as staging posts for coaches. Further out from London the same was true for such places as Godstone, Cuckfield and Handcross. In their day the coach roads, particularly the new ones as some of the Brighton roads were, changed the places they passed through every bit as much as the railways were to do in the second half of the nineteenth century.

The height of the coaching era, the 'Golden Age' when coaching reached its peak of excellence, was attained only from approximately 1824 to 1848, yet it has bequeathed a lasting legacy of romantic images. The coaches have ceased to ply our roads, but they still grace many a Christmas card and are an inescapable ingredient of any costume drama we watch on television.

The legacy of the coaching age is not just an image on a screen, however. The roads to Brighton have been subjected to an almost continuous tide of change as the ever-advancing demands of modernity spread across the land, but much still remains unchanged.

An obvious example is seen on those Christmas card pictures in which the coach is often seen standing outside an inn. The coach may now have gone but a good number of the old inns still survive. They still stand beside the road along which the coaches came and may often be recognised by the presence of an archway through which coaches passed to reach the yard and the stabling beyond. Many are ancient buildings, survivors from long before the Golden Age, with low-beamed ceilings and a cheerful fire to greet the traveller if the weather is cold. Others were built especially to serve the increasing traffic which the growth of Brighton had generated. In either case the traveller is attracted, perhaps unconsciously, by the historic ambience of the place. Many have survived precisely because the wise innkeeper knows the value of the atmosphere in attracting custom.

If buildings along the road remind us of its past, this is perhaps even more true of Brighton itself. Here are fine Georgian buildings and the famous area known as the Lanes, where much remains that would have pleased those visitors who had recently alighted from their coaches, and which still pleases us today. Brighton has also that wonderful but preposterous edifice, the Brighton Pavilion, which is certainly eye-catching and symbolises the excessive extravagance of Regency England. It is a building that epitomises perfectly an age of extremes of fashion and ostentatious wealth in the top echelons of society.

The different Brighton roads come together at the place which was then the heart of coaching in the town: Castle Square. Day and night it was a centre of bustle and noise, smelling of horses and constantly reverberating to the passage of coach wheels. Today this is one spot that has little remaining from those exciting times. It seems empty; a much-changed relic of a place that could not survive the loss of its lifeblood: the coaches that used to flow through it.

Where the roads started in London, however, there is still more than enough noise and traffic. Nearly all the inns from which the coaches started their journeys have now gone but, to go south, much of the modern traffic still follows the old coach routes. Coaches for Brighton crossed the Thames over London Bridge or Westminster Bridge and headed south to where the two roads met at Kennington. From here they spread out by numerous bifurcating routes and eventually met again at Brighton.

The story of the Brighton roads can be gathered from the printed page and from investigation along the roads themselves. The first reference for anyone studying the subject has to be Charles Harper's *The Brighton Road*. This is a fascinating book that was published at the end of the nineteenth century. It is a thoroughly entertaining account of much that happened on the road and, most importantly, it tells where precisely the main route ran; when it was built or when turned into a turnpike. Harper was able to talk to people who remembered the road in its heyday and, of course, lived in an age when much travel by horse-drawn vehicle was still the norm. Harper's book is a goldmine of information but, for him, there was just one main route: that which ran directly south from London through Croydon. Reigate, Crawley and Cuckfield, then through the Pyecombe Gap in the South Downs to Brighton. He shows various deviations from this route and includes a map to indicate where these were. The dates when the different parts were turnpiked are accurately recorded. This route was undoubtedly the most important but Harper scarcely acknowledges that it was never the only way to Brighton. Other ways, of great importance, he completely overlooked. One road went through Horsham and Steyning, another through East Grinstead. These were important courses to the south coast long before the growth of Brighton had stimulated new road construction on the more direct route. These roads continued to be used and adapted and are still perfectly good ways to get to Brighton today. There were also a number of other minor routes regularly used by coaches.

These other routes have not been accounted for in books in the same detail that Harper gave to the major road, but there are still records that provide valuable information. Some are general accounts, for example *Brighton and its Coaches* by W. C. A. Blew. This was, like Harper's text, published at the end of the nineteenth century. Other accounts, notably J. Edwards' *A Companion from London to Brighthelmstone in Sussex*, are personal accounts of a journey to Brighton written in the coaching age. There are also, of course, many records in local histories which, when put together, provide another rich source of information. Precise identification of the position of roadside buildings, such as toll gates, is given on the tithe maps of the 1840s and the first edition of the Ordnance Survey 25-inches-to-the-mile maps.

As you would expect, the libraries of London provide a rich source of information about coach roads, particularly at their

London end. Fine pictures pertaining to the Brighton roads may be found in the British Library and also in the London Metropolitan Archives. Useful books are available in the Minet Library in Lambeth, for example *Turnpikes and Toll Bars* by Mark Searl. This two-volume book must have been a labour of love for Mr Searl, a man of extreme patience who seems to have looked through every newspaper and journal he could find nationwide and recorded all the references to toll gates. Two more recent books, Anthony Bird's *Roads and Vehicles* and David Mountfield's *The Coaching Age*, are invaluable for detail on the coaches themselves. They give the reader a clear vision of the nature of road traffic in the coaching era; traffic which contrasts so greatly to that of the present day.

If, today, you wish to find out when trains or buses are leaving for your destination and what places they will pass through, you look them up in a timetable. The same applied to coach travellers. Even the wealthy individual in his own carriage would follow the better-engineered roads on the main routes and these were generally the roads followed by the stage coaches. Off these routes there was always the danger of getting lost, and only on the main roads could the traveller be sure to find refreshment and, most importantly, a change of horses.

Modern train journeys south depart from only a few main stations such as Charing Cross and London Bridge. Coach companies started their journeys from city inns, and a great many of these were used. The coach horses were usually stabled at the inns from which the coach departed. Since coach departures were often at an unseasonably early hour, intending passengers could be accommodated at the inn overnight. One major 'timetable' for coaches was *Cary's Roads*, which included "A list of inns throughout the metropolis from which the Mail and other Stage Coaches depart". As an example, the list for 1817 shows that Brighton was very well served by coaches. Cary lists 16 different London inns from which coaches left for Brighton. The Golden Cross, at Charing Cross, was the departure point for a multitude of coaches. Among them was the "original red coach", leaving daily at 10am and arriving at Brighton at 6pm. It went through "Croydon, Ryegate, Crawley and Cuckfield". This was clearly the most popular route for many coaches, but certainly not the only one. The Brighton coach which left the Bolt-in-Tun, Fleet Street, at eight in the morning passed "thro' Dorking, Horsham and Steyning" and a similar route was followed by the *Royal Clarence* from the Bull, Bishopsgate Street. However from the Vine, also in Bishopsgate Street, three alternative routes were available, through 'Reygate' and Crawley, through Dorking and Horsham and finally by way of Croydon, Godstone, East Grinstead, Uckfield and Lewes.

These timetabled routes serve well to define the coach roads to Brighton. Of all these roads, the first to be recognised as an important route to Brighton was the one that passed through Croydon, Godstone and East Grinstead. This was the London to Lewes road, which had been an important route for many centuries and which, in part, followed the Roman London–Lewes Way. It was extended as a turnpike road from Lewes to Brighton when the growth of the latter town started to generate sufficient traffic.

Considerably further west is another Brighton road which, like the Lewes route, did not originally lead to Brighton but was extended to that town as it grew in importance. This road linked London to such towns as Epsom, Leatherhead and Dorking. From here it ran south to Horsham and then split, with one branch reaching Brighton through Steyning and another through Henfield. Like the way through East Grinstead, this road was not discussed by Harper.

Between these two roads are the roads which Harper does describe, the Brighton roads par excellence and the most direct ways to Brighton. These roads were the precursors of the modern A23 and M23 and were developed later than the Lewes and Horsham routes. The most famous of them ran through Sutton and Reigate to Crawley and then through Handcross, Cuckfield and Clayton. This road, often referred to as the Classic Route, rapidly became the premier Brighton road. It took about as direct a course as was possible, fifty-one and a half miles, and in about 1790 was named by Shergold as "The Appian Way for the High Nobility of England". This was indeed one of the major roads for Regency England, with the number of splendid carriages using it eclipsing even those of the other fashionable road, the Bath Road. This route to Brighton was the scene of many notable coaching events, and records were set for fast passage of the distance by different types of coaches just as they were later by cyclists and walkers. Even in the motoring age the road has maintained its hold on the imagination and is the scene of the Brighton Run of old cars immortalised in the film *Genevieve*.

The Classic route had two important additions made to it. In 1808 a new road was opened between Foxley Hatch, the present

Purley, and Reigate. It cut through the village of Merstham and replaced the many winding lanes around that village. In 1816 this new road was extended south to Povey Cross, just to the north of what is now Gatwick Airport. The road bypassed Reigate and went through open country where Redhill now stands. In 1813 another new road was made, this time between Handcross and Pyecombe via Hickstead. The total length of the route was now even shorter as it avoided the twisting road to Cuckfield. Both these variations are part of the present A23 road and carry a lot of the traffic between London and Brighton, particularly on the Hickstead section which serves as a continuation of the M23 motorway.

Other 'minor' but still important routes to Brighton were the road from Horley down to Cuckfield, and that from Newchapel through Turners Hill, Lindfield and Ditchling. This is the prettiest of all the Brighton roads but may have been less favoured because it included the steep ascent of the South Downs to Ditchling Beacon.

To anyone reading about old roads it soon becomes apparent what a vital part of our nation's history the coach roads were. Other forms of transport played their part – rivers and the sea could be used to move goods if the goods concerned were near them – but the roads were the arteries along which the lifeblood of the nation moved. They are still arteries of course, although increasingly sclerotic, but today there are the alternatives of rail and air. At the height of the coaching age you went by coach or on horseback or you walked, unless you happened to live near suitable water transport. The development of the coach road exactly mirrored the development of the nation through the industrial age. Perhaps this fact has been partly responsible for the romance of the coach road to modern eyes. Perhaps it is simply that any widespread activity that has now gone becomes suffused with a romantic aura that ignores all the disadvantages and hardships that were readily apparent at the time. Now we see the same phenomenon amongst the devotees of steam railways, or feel it when treading the decks of Nelson's flagship *Victory* at Portsmouth. Pictures of a bygone countryside and words written about a past age can easily over-romanticise the harsh reality of the time that is portrayed.

Certainly many of the coaching roads developed a fame and indeed a character of their own; a character derived from the places they passed through and from the legendary people and events associated with them. There is romance in their very names and, in particular, with the great roads out from London. The Dover Road, gateway to the continent; the Bath Road, carriageway for the *haut ton* of Regency England; the Portsmouth Road, highway to the port and the greatest navy the world had seen; and the longest of all, the Great North Road, stretching through the best part of the length of the kingdom. Yet the road to Brighton, little over 50 miles though it might have been, had as great a claim to eminence as any of the others and was frequently travelled by the royalty, nobility and gentry of the nation. Coach companies vied for domination, while towns and villages along the route flourished by serving the travellers' needs. Brighton became something approaching a coastal suburb of London, a status it still holds today, 150 years after the passing of the coaching age.

Add together the length of the various old roads linking London and Brighton and they come to about two hundred miles. For almost every place along those routes someone has written about its local history, including its roads. The record offices of Surrey and East and West Sussex contain many interesting documents and detailed maps, while old prints show the coaches themselves. All are very important, but there is another resource that unites the various items into a coherent whole. That resource is to be found along the roads themselves. It is seen in the surrounding countryside, the roadside buildings that have survived from the coaching age and the nature of the land over which the roads wind their way. This resource cannot be researched in a library; nor can it be observed from a car window. The only way is to walk every one of those two hundred miles, whether they are busy main roads or quiet green tracks; to walk through an ancient landscape where, in times gone by, the coaches swayed, the horses sweated and Regency England followed its prince to the seaside at Brighton.

Plate 1

A sandy track on Ashdown Forest. The surface in the High Weald easily broke down. Valleys were avoided where possible by keeping to the high land between river basins. Many coach roads were little better than this track.

Plate 2

The old coach road up Beeding Hill. Despite the steep gradients involved, the firm dry surface of the chalk was preferred to the damp land in the valleys. Small patches of the old surface of packed flints still survive.

Plate 3

The Cock at Sutton. This inn has now gone, but many other old inns on the Brighton roads still survive. They were essential for rest and refreshment and, above all, for changing horses.

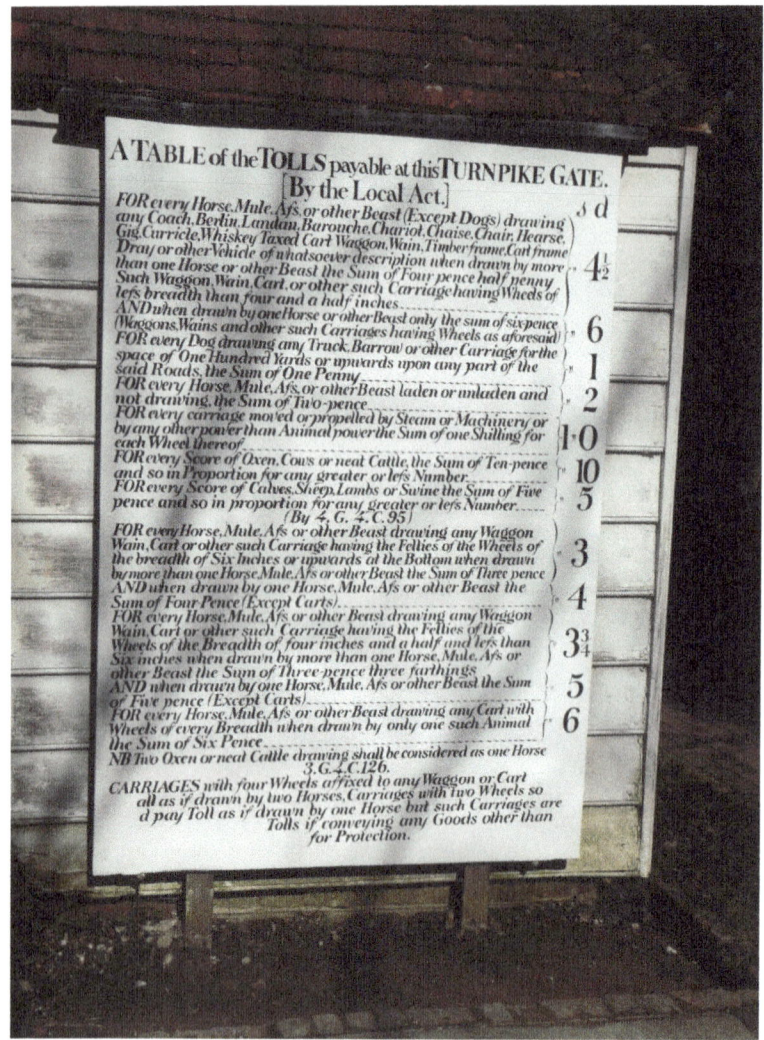

Plate 4

The toll board from Beeding toll house. Tolls were charged to fund maintenance of the turnpike roads and to give some return on their investment to the trustees.

Plate 5

The Brighton Pavilion is the iconic symbol of Regency Brighton, the growth of which town led to the development of the coach roads south from London.

Chapter 2
The Lewes Route: London to Streatham

Most coaches leaving London for the south crossed the Thames either by London Bridge or Westminster Bridge. With the growth of Brighton as a haunt of the nobility, Westminster Bridge became the preferred crossing as it was the obvious route for the wealthy residents of the West End. However, the older coach routes to such places as Horsham and Lewes had been important for centuries during which the small fishing village of Brighthelmstone had not yet been transformed into Brighton. There was no call for the major coaching proprietors to run a service over the barrier of the South Downs to the coast, and services stopped at the inland towns.

Westminster Bridge was not opened until November 10th 1750 so the older roads started by crossing London Bridge, and this crossing continued to be important throughout the coaching age. As Brighton developed however, Westminster Bridge carried an increasing amount of traffic and many of the surviving milestones on the roads to Brighton are inscribed with the distance to this crossing. One splendid milestone serving the Westminster Bridge traffic can still be seen standing outside the Imperial War Museum. It is a large obelisk, far grander than a normal milestone, and is engraved with the distances to London Bridge, Palace Yard, Westminster Hall and Fleet Street. It used to stand near St. George's Circus and was erected in 1771 when Blackfriars Road and London Road were built over an area which until that time had remained as open fields. It serves as a reminder that milestones were important markers on the old roads, and is also a reminder of how comparatively recently London has developed beyond the area of Southwark south of the river. It is hard to visualise that there were still fields in this area as recently as 1771!

In the early days of Brighton coaches, the road through Lewes was the only route, and London Bridge was the Thames crossing that most companies used. As other routes developed, this crossing remained the preference of many companies because it was so favourably positioned for the use of coaches based in the city. Across the river came coaches from the Blossoms Inn, Cheapside, the White Horse in Fetter Lane, the Bull, the George, the Bell and Crown, the Blue Boar in Holborn and the Angel in the Strand. Some of these were very large establishments, the equivalent of large railway terminals today. The Bull and Mouth, in St. Martin's Le Grand, had underground stables large enough to accommodate four hundred horses. The splendid sign from this inn, a huge smiling mouth surmounted by a bull, is now displayed in the museum of London. The Bull and Mouth was associated with one of the most famous of all Brighton coaches, the *Age*. *Cary's Roads* shows us that, in 1817, passengers wishing to travel to Lewes should book a place on a coach from the Golden Cross at Charing Cross, but by this date the continuation to Brighton had been abandoned in favour of the more direct route. Only from the Vine, in Bishopsgate Street, could you book a coach through to Brighton via Lewes.

The inns must have varied in quality. They were certainly very noisy, and would have suffered, even more than London as a whole, from the all-pervading smell of horses. The Golden Cross was one of the most important inns for departure to Brighton. Many coaches left from here but the management seem to have adopted a cavalier attitude towards the comfort of intending passengers. In his account of a journey in about 1790 Shergold refers to this inn as "a nasty inn, remarkable for filth and apparent misery". Most inns did nevertheless provide a good service for their customers, and some of them were much better than others. In 1801 Edwards wrote of the Spread Eagle in Gracechurch Street:

> "... a large and noted inn, at which many stage coaches put up. Also it is worthy of notice for the number and excellence of its beds. Here are about fifty lodging rooms, mostly single bedded, kept very clean, and the furniture genteel; decent people coming here, though at a late hour, are seldom disappointed of being agreeably accommodated with a bed, and in

general no more charged than one shilling per night."

The timetable for 1817 shows that two coaches left the Spread Eagle for Brighton every day: the *Comet* at ten in the morning and the *Dart* at 1.45 in the afternoon. Presumably Mr Edwards left on the *Comet* after a night in his clean and comfortable bed.

If, by the height of the coaching age, a passenger needed to follow the old Brighton road and travel via Lewes, he would book a coach from the Vine and probably stay overnight. This would leave time for breakfast before the coach departed at seven in the morning ("Sundays excepted"). The coach, full of passengers, either sleepy or well-breakfasted, would make its way down Gracechurch Street and so over London Bridge and down Borough High Street. Much of this is a fairly undistinguished street today and it did not appear particularly remarkable to Edwards when he travelled down it in 1801. The roadsides he describes were, however, very different from their appearance two hundred years later. In 1801 they must have presented quite an animated scene, with great cartloads of produce coming in from the countryside. The west side of the road was principally occupied by butchers, and the east side by hop factors. These activities have long since ceased to function in the area, but one building does remain; a building which Edwards does not mention, presumably because it was to him just another inn. This is the George Inn, a surviving gem of the coaching age

The George stands on the eastern side of the road, at number 77, and is one of the treasures of London. It is the last remaining galleried inn in London and is now owned by the National Trust but leased to a private company who use it as a public house. It was a well-known coaching inn and was mentioned by Charles Dickens in *Little Dorrit*. The building dates from 1677 and its rooms overlook a cobbled courtyard. Many of the London inns were built in this way, with galleries outside the rooms overlooking the courtyard below but, apart from the George, they have all gone. There were originally three sides to the building but, at one time, the Great Northern Railway used the George as a depot and two sides were pulled down to make way for warehousing, although thankfully the southern side survived. Intending passengers would have been able to relax on the galleries and look down on a lively and constantly changing scene below. The cobbles are still there where hundreds of coaches must have discharged their passengers, and inside are passages and rooms with low ceilings and heavy beams. It seems only right that there is a Dickensian connection as the whole place is so much of that period. It may no longer be redolent of clay pipes and rush lamps; it may lack the jingle of harnesses as horses toss their heads in the courtyard, but it is certainly a place in which to linger with pleasure, particularly inside the building where the sound of modern traffic is less intrusive.

Borough High Street must once have teemed with coaches. Many would have swung left into Great Dover Street, heading for the Old Kent Road and the coach roads to Canterbury and Dover. The southbound coaches continued to Newington Causeway and so to the Elephant and Castle. Then, as now, this was a difficult crossroads as the Kent-bound coaches crossed the north to south road. Combine the number of coaches with narrow ancient roads and the unpredictability of horseflesh, and the scene must have been lively to say the least! The problem with such major road junctions for those wishing to understand what they were like in the past is that, over the years, no one can leave them alone. Even more so than Borough High Street, the Elephant and Castle has been changed again and again so that nothing of coaching interest remains. Beyond this was the road beside Kennington Park, leading coaches to what was probably the best known and most notorious toll gate in all of south London: Kennington Gate.

Before reaching the site of the gate, the road passes Kennington Park, the first piece of open land to be found beside the road. It was enclosed as a park in 1851, but before that, and through most of the coaching years, it was the unfenced expanse of Kennington Common. Already, at this early stage of the journey, the truly urban environment was starting to be left behind. Just before the gate, the roads from Westminster Bridge and London Bridge come together at the junction with Kennington Road. Milestones down the roads heading south acknowledge the two sources of the road. Many give distances to London as the number of miles to Cornhill in the City; others give the distance to Westminster Bridge. Some give both.

Kennington Gate stood to the south-west corner of the park, and Brighton coaches passed through it to follow Clapham Road for the Horsham and Classic routes, or Brixton Road for the way through Lewes. With all this traffic the area was always busy and if there is one place on the Brighton coach road that is well reported and illustrated it is Kennington Gate!

The Metropolitan Archives have a lot of useful information about this area. It includes some fine pictures of coaches that travelled the Brighton road, and also a photograph of Kennington Gate taken shortly before its final removal. There are four illustrations of Kennington Gate in *Turnpikes and Toll Bars*, one of which shows Kennington in 1842 when the open land was still common. The western side of the road is built up, and St. Mark's Church is prominent. The common is separated from the road by a simple wooden fence, behind which a group of young ladies are sitting on the grass having a picnic as some cows graze in the background. Other pictures show the toll house; an octagonal building standing in the middle of the broad road with gates on either side of it. Although busy for its time, the area around the gate looks quiet to modern eyes. A later picture, from 1865, shows one heavily-laden cart coming steadily through the gate, while a workman stands at the side of the road and some men with time on their hands are chatting to each other beside the gatehouse.

There were days in the year, however, when the traffic at Kennington Gate became as busy, and perhaps even more hectic, than modern London. One of these was the day of Croydon Fair and, even more so, Derby Day, when the press of carriages became quite chaotic. A picture taken from the *Pictorial Times* of June 3rd 1843 shows a Derby Day scene verging on the disastrous. Some horsemen have galloped across in front of a heavily overladen coach, the horses of which are rearing and near to falling. A boy has fallen on his back in the road, the roof passengers are crying out in alarm and some pedestrians are almost crushed between the coach and the adjacent fence. Every type of vehicle packed the roads to Epsom on Derby Day, and another illustration of 1843 shows seven different vehicles apparently hurtling past the gate, with clouds of dust thrown up by their wheels. A typically lively Cruikshank drawing depicts people returning from the races in 1837. Coachmen are brandishing their whips, shouting and gesticulating; urchins fight with each other while spectators crowd around, get in the way and make comments, probably caustic and certainly unhelpful.

Like all toll gates, the Kennington Gate was heartily disliked by the majority who passed through it. In an age of minimal taxation the cost of the toll and the inconvenience of the gates was felt to be an imposition. The Kennington Gate was finally removed on

October 31st 1865, and the *Illustrated London News* of December 9th commented that the gate was "one of the most familiar objects in the experience of the Londoner". It went on to say that "its final disappearance, though not an occasion of regret, must be noticed as a sign of the rapid changes of this busy and improving age".

Pictures of cattle grazing on the common, or even the exciting bustle of Derby Day, must be set against a darker side of life when the coaches passed through Kennington. The site of St. Mark's Church, like the site of the toll gate itself, was once part of Kennington Common and was a favoured place for executions. According to Edwards it was "the common place of execution for the county of Surrey". The remains of the original gibbet were discovered when the foundations of the church were being excavated. In the present rather dull surroundings of the church it is almost impossible to imagine the main feature of the road here to be a great gibbet, or that instead of the smell of car fumes there would have been the smell of rotting flesh. There certainly seems to have been no lack of work for the gibbet. One group of people who ended their days on display here were some of the rebels from the 1745 Jacobite rebellion.

One notorious highwayman whose body was hanged in chains at Kennington was Jerry Abershaw, described as a "debonair crepe-masked highwayman, who was remarkable for his audacity". He was eventually brought to trial in Croydon on the two charges of having shot and murdered David Price, a law officer, and having fired at Bernard Turner, another officer, with intent to murder him. He escaped conviction on the murder charge due to a flaw in the indictment but was convicted on the second charge, which was also punishable by death. When the judge put on his black cap, Abershaw put on his hat and looked at the judge with "supreme contempt". He was taken to Kennington for execution and during the journey kept up a constant conversation, laughing and nodding to spectators and seeming quite unconcerned. He was hanged on 3rd August 1795; his body remaining in place as a warning to others and becoming, for a time, a familiar sight to travellers on the road. Today it is hard to imagine whether coach travellers found the sight reassuring or revolting.

The coach travelling to Brighton through Lewes would have crossed the River Effra by a bridge immediately south of Kennington Church, and gone by way of Brixton Road and Brixton Hill. Brixton is now a busy place with a bustling cosmopolitan population, utterly different from how it was two centuries ago. It was a pretty place during the coaching era, as the River Effra flowed down the eastern side of the road. This was a typical chalk stream some 12 feet wide, and quite deep. Wells in the area were said to have a mineral quality: beer made from their waters would 'purge'. Houses by the road were, at that time, reached by little bridges across the stream. The river still remains but has long been confined underground. Its name, however, remains in Effra Road. A number of the Georgian houses standing here may well have been standing when the river flowed along in front of them. Such houses would have been attractive dwellings for early commuters to London, who could come home at night to a quiet, leafy environment.

Travellers south through Brixton to Croydon would have been very aware of the landscape around them as they finally emerged from the built-up area into the true countryside. Much was farmland but there was also wooded heath, cut through by sandy tracks; dusty in summer and muddy in winter. The main road climbs the hills on fairly gentle gradients but it is only when you walk up them that you realise how significant were the inclines of Brixton Hill and Streatham Hill for coaches. Horses pulling a well-laden coach up the loose surface of the road would have had to work hard. A modern driver along these roads would probably never even notice the hills.

The woodland and heath of the countryside south of Kennington was a mixed blessing to coach travellers. The fresh air may have been welcome, but the area was well suited to the activities of highwaymen. There was plenty of cover for these gentlemen all the way to Brighton, but robbery was much more frequent on the roads near London because of the greater amount of traffic there, and the presence of more people with sufficient wealth to make them worth robbing. If the highwayman did not ambush you, there were plenty of other mishaps that could occur. Accidents involving coaches, like car accidents today, were an ever-present danger on the road. It seems that the more reports of coaching traffic that you read, the more you hear of death and disaster. Presumably the same will be true for anyone in the next century reading reports of traffic on our roads. Then, as now, a safe journey was not news.

Accidents were quite likely. The behaviour of horses is even more unpredictable than that of car drivers and there were many points in the structure of carts and carriages which could fail as a result of wear and tear, or of overloading. It was the overloading of a coach that caused an accident in Brixton on June 25th 1810. Waldegrave's accommodation coach was near Brixton Causeway on its way to London, and so heavily loaded that the rear wheels suddenly collapsed from the excess weight and the coach overturned. The passengers survived due to a circumstance that would certainly not occur in Brixton today: a farmer's wagon was passing at the very moment of the overturn, and was presumably loaded with something soft such as hay. The outside passengers, thrown off the coach, landed in the wagon. They received bruises, and one man suffered a broken leg, but worse disaster was prevented.

At the junction of Brixton Road and Effra Road there is a square pillar of sandstone, the first of many milestones still standing on the Brighton road. It gives a distance of four miles to the Royal Exchange; information relevant to those coaches which had come from the City via London Bridge. How very different are its surroundings now compared to when it was first erected! This place was then at the very edge of the London suburbs, where the true countryside began.

Rush Common is now the only tiny remnant of open land to have survived beside the road – all else is a totally built-up environment. This common was larger in coaching days, with the River Effra meandering across it. For the slow-moving coaches, particularly in the eighteenth century before coach design and road surfaces had been improved, the area was one where danger could always lurk. The rural surroundings offered excellent cover for highwaymen and the coaches were an easy target. One such highwayman, Jack Gutteridge, who operated on this part of the road during the 1720s, subsequently spent further time beside it hanging on a gibbet which stood opposite the fifth milestone in Streatham. He was executed for robbing and murdering a gentleman's servant at this spot and his body was left hanging in chains at the scene of his crime. Presumably a highwayman knew that if he was caught he was likely to be publicly hanged. Did this knowledge deter him? Clearly not in the case of Mr Gutteridge! History has invested such people with a certain glamour, but there can have been little glamour when hiding amongst the trees of Streatham Common and eking out a living from the meagre pickings coach travellers afforded.

The coach that had left Bishopsgate at seven in the morning would almost certainly have given its horses a short rest at Streatham, and the arrival at the village would have provided a welcome break. It was described as "a pleasant village, and allowed to be remarkably healthy". Streatham was sometimes used as a staging post where teams of horses were changed and passengers could refresh themselves, particularly those who had left London without breakfast! It was too near London to be used as more than a refreshment stop for most coaches, however; they went through to make their first change at Croydon. Horses could be obtained in Streatham from the Pied Bull, the White Lion and from the Horse and Groom, previously known as the Halfway House as it lay halfway between London and Croydon. Few features of the coaching age remain as the inn was rebuilt in 1865. It continued to house horses for many years and the service given lost none of its efficiency with the passage of time. It provided one of the fastest changes for John Selby, who made a famous drive in 1888. The Horse and Groom was a favourite stopping place for the Prince Regent on his journeys to Brighton. He would partake of refreshment there and enjoy gambling, and also cock fighting which was laid on especially for him.

A milestone survives on the east of Streatham High Road, giving distances of six miles to the Royal Exchange and five and a half to Whitehall. This is one of a whole series set up at the very height of the coaching age in about 1830. The two London destinations show the continuing relevance of both the London Bridge and Westminster Bridge routes across the Thames.

A great variety of different types of coaches passed through Streatham every day. It was a busy and thriving place, gaining much benefit from its services to the passing coaches. On a busy road like this every type of vehicle might be seen. There was the local traffic of farm carts, traps and gigs. There were the splendid carriages of the nobility and gentry, and the smaller but faster phaetons and curricles. Some of the smartest of all were the resplendent mail coaches, surely the lords of the road in their day. Yet, despite this multiplicity of vehicles, the essence of the coaching age and the backbone of the transport system was the stage coach.

The romance of the stage coach is such that a vast literature exists on the subject, and the appearance of the coach is familiar from many a television drama. However, there was never just one model of stage coach. The coaches evolved, as modern cars have evolved, to reflect advancing technological skills and changing public needs. The earlier stage coaches, up to about 1790, were cumbrous and uncomfortable and needed a team of six horses to pull them. Construction was based on a large beam, known as the perch, which was something like the keel of a ship with other parts attached to it. The axle beds were fastened to it, with the fore axle being pivoted on a bolt: the perch bolt that linked it to the perch. Various methods were used to link the axle to the shafts, but the perch bolt was always a point of weakness. It was under constant strain and if the rear wheels came up against an obstacle, not an unusual eventuality with deeply rutted roads, the bolt could break and the horses would then pull the fore wheels away from the rest of the coach, which would probably overturn.

Above this massive but potentially insecure base, the body of the coach was made particularly unstable by its height above the ground. The rear wheels were five feet six inches in diameter, so the coach had to be suspended two feet above the perch in order to allow the doors to open clear of the wheels. The floor of the coach was thus at least four feet from the ground. These massive vehicles, quite often made even heavier by being overloaded with passengers, must nevertheless have been an impressive sight as they lumbered past. For the passengers, however, the journey was one of great discomfort. They were closely packed into a small and probably smelly compartment, which swayed considerably on various types of suspension. Improvements were made to this over the years and passengers were gradually protected from the worst joltings over the road, but the motion must have made many people feel extremely unwell.

Fore and aft of the main body, the early coaches were not sprung in any way at all. The fore boot and the driver's box seat were mounted directly onto the perch above the front axles, which resulted in the coachman having a very uncomfortable ride indeed. Coach proprietors felt this was an advantage as it kept the coachman awake and alert. The box seat was, of course, at a lower level than the body of the coach. This restricted the coachman's view of his horses and meant that if more than a pair of horses was used, the leaders had to be controlled by a postillion. At the rear of the coach, in the days before a boot had been developed, there was the basket, a wicker-work construction known also as the rumble-tumble. Fastened to iron stays between the back wheels it was originally intended for luggage but it became the custom to allow the very poorest passengers to travel in it. Such people were conveyed in the most extreme discomfort, being jolted against the coach and the axle and with their bruises scarcely cushioned by the provision of a supply of hay in the bottom of the basket. Even to this day the term "in the basket" may be heard in relation to someone with serious problems.

The roof was a little more comfortable than the basket but, until nearly 1800, not much more so. The coach roof at this time was curved and nothing apart from a handle was provided to hold on to, and as no boot existed there were no footholds, yet coachmen would often, for a small consideration, agree to let unofficial passengers ride on the roof. To journey on such a seat, above a lurching coach, breathing in the dust of the road and exposed to all the vagaries of the weather, must only have been possible for the hardiest and most athletic of passengers. Inside passengers were equally jolted, and often uncomfortably crowded, but were at least protected from the elements and had no fear of falling from the roof.

From the end of the eighteenth century a number of technical innovations did much to improve the quality of coach travel for coachmen and passengers alike. The introduction of swingletrees, bars attached to the coach by swivel hooks, gave the coachman much better control over his horses, but the most important change for passengers was the use of semi-elliptical steel springs, developed by Obediah Elliot in 1804, which replaced the crude suspension straps that had previously been used. The idea of their introduction is thought to have been suggested by John Warde of Squerryes in Kent. He was one of the very first amateur coachmen and found, from personal experience, how excessively uncomfortable the driver's seat was. The introduction of a much improved suspension system was greeted as a revolutionary and invaluable advance in coach design. With effective and reliably strong springing, the front boot and box seat could now be fastened to the body of the coach while the basket was replaced by the hind boot, matching the coachman's box in front, and also fastened to the coach body. The springs beneath the coach now rested directly on the axels and so eliminated the need for the perch. A coach journey was now much more comfortable for both drivers and passengers – no longer were their spines jolted over every rut in the road. Apart from comfort, the great advantage of the new design was that the centre of gravity was lowered, making an overturn much less likely. Conversely, the coachman himself was now seated higher up with a much better view, which meant that he could control the whole team of horses himself. Many of the improvements in coach construction, such as improved springing, were first adopted by the mail coaches and only gradually became commonplace on stage coaches also.

There are many hills on the roads to Brighton and control of the coach on these was, of course, particularly important. On an uphill journey the coach was prevented from careering backwards downhill again primarily by the strength of the horses. They were helped, however, when ascending steep hills by the drag staff, or sprag. This was a rod attached by a hinge to the hind axel tree so that it would be dragged along the road at the rear of the coach, and would dig in if the vehicle slid backwards. It could be raised if the coach was being backed deliberately.

The strength of the coachman and horses, particularly the wheelers, was the main safety factor when going downhill. Of the four horses, the wheelers were the two nearest the coach and would feel the full weight of it behind them. They were, however, assisted by the shoe, or skid pan. This looked something like a small shovel and was attached by a chain to the side of the coach. When descending hills, it was the guard's duty to place the shoe under one of the rear wheels so that the coach ran on three wheels and the shoe, and was slowed accordingly. Some skill was needed in placing the shoe in the right position. It was certainly not a fully reliable method and, if the shoe broke on a steep hill, the horses would be unable to hold the coach and would have to gallop for it. This must have been a terrifying experience as, if the horses completely lost control, the horses, coach and all who were in it ended up as a pile of wreckage at the foot of the hill. Handbrakes were not fitted until 1835, and were strongly opposed by many professional coachmen who were proud of their skill and considered brakes to be only of use in helping amateurs.

The old heavy coaches had carried six inside passengers, but the new vehicles normally carried four although a couple more could be squeezed in. Better design had certainly made coaches safer and more comfortable, but comfort is a relative term and car passengers today would still consider them very uncomfortable indeed. Although the inside passengers were shielded from the weather they had little other comfort on their journey. They had to sit bolt upright, their knees nearly touched those of the passengers on the opposite seats and the small compartment soon became very stuffy. The number of outside passengers was originally limited to three, but better design gave rise to a rapid increase in this number. The flat roofs of the new coaches provided seats for three rear passengers, another three in front and one on the box seat next to the driver. The rear boot supported a forward-facing seat for passengers and the guard, and a footrest for the backward-facing passengers on the seat at the rear of the roof. The seats were narrow, with little padding, and the backrest was only a low iron rail.

As always seems to be the case, the advantageous new conditions were soon the subject of abuse, the most obvious of which was overloading. A safer coach soon became thoroughly unsafe again if too many people piled onto the roof. That this sometimes happened to excess, even with the very unstable old coaches, is illustrated by a letter to the *Times* in April 1795. The writer had observed a coach at the Obelisk in St. George's Fields which had "fourteen passengers on the roof of the coach, some of whom were soldiers, five in the basket, and two with the coachman on the box, making, with six inside passengers and one child, in the whole twenty eight passengers!" The writer does not say how the horses were able to get this monstrous equipage into motion at all, but it seems doubtful that they could have moved it very far.

The problem of overloading was well known to those in authority and, in 1788, Gammon's Act was passed which limited the number of roof passengers to six, but as the above shows, it was widely ignored. Turnpike keepers were supposed to collect a five-shilling fine for each illegally loaded coach passing through their gate but they often came to an arrangement with the coachman. It was almost impossible to enforce the law on overloading, particularly on country routes. Many coachmen were only too happy to squeeze a few more passengers onto the roof, as the extra fares paid were a useful additional income. One simple way of avoiding the fine was for the passengers to get down and walk through the gate and then climb aboard again once the coach had safely passed through with a legal load.

Rewards were offered where information led to a conviction, and this led to informers making a living from reporting overloaded coaches. The best known of these was a man named Byers who operated across southern England. Thanks to his activities numbers of convictions were obtained, but many of his 'informations' were petty. For example, one Brighton coach was reported for having its name painted in the wrong place. It may, in any case, have been difficult to read the name as coaches were often painted with many garish colours to make them stand out from the crowd. Despite the dangerous state of some coaches, informers as a race were heartily disliked.

Coaches were often made ridiculously high and unstable, not so much with passengers but with luggage. Small items of luggage could be carried in the boot but there was no room there for large items, which had to be carried on the roof. Other bundles would be tied on to any available place, such as the lamp brackets. So much luggage could find its way to the roof that an Act was passed in 1811 prohibiting roof luggage rising to more than eight feet nine inches from the ground where the gauge of the coach was under four foot six inches. There is some cause to wonder how even a coach within this legal limit, made further unstable by passengers on the roof, ever remained upright long enough to finish its journey. Clearly passengers were not reluctant to ride on the roof, despite the dangers and discomforts of such a position. On a fine day it must have been much pleasanter out in the fresh air, yet the danger of an overturn could be very real. In adverse weather conditions the cold and wet were serious matters. There are even records of roof passengers being frozen to death, as happened to two people who travelled through the night in March 1812. This was not on the Brighton road but still in southern England, on the road to Chippenham. Stage coach journeys were often cancelled in very bad weather (with good reason, it would seem), but the mails tried to run whatever the conditions.

Of course there were as many variations in the design of coaches as there are in public vehicles today, and old slow coaches still kept the road long after they had been superseded by new designs. The old coaches would carry those with less money, those of a nervous disposition, or those in less of a hurry than passengers in the newest coaches. The faster coaches often had names which implied characteristics of speed, for example the *Alert* or the *Quicksilver*. Others appealed to patriotic instincts with names such as the *True Blue* or the *Sovereign*. Two general terms were frequently used. A Machine was a common name for coaches from 1754 to 1800. It was probably just a light stage coach. An Accommodation coach was a slow stage coach, common all over the country from about

1800. It provided ample room and stopped frequently to set down and pick up passengers or luggage.

The cost of a journey in a stage coach was considerably less than in a hired vehicle and depended on whereabouts on the coach you sat. The fare from London to Brighton in 1770 was 14 shillings for an inside passenger, and luggage over one stone in weight cost a penny a pound. By 1808 fares at one office were 23 shillings inside and 13 shillings outside. Growing competition reduced these fares and by 1814 a journey to Brighton by the *Regent* coach cost ten shillings inside and five shillings outside.

Before the second half of the eighteenth century coaches could not really be called stage coaches at all. The great lumbering vehicles of the period were pulled by the same team, usually of six horses, for the entire journey. The 'stage' was merely the interval between each stop and passengers had to wait perforce, until the horses were sufficiently rested. The true 'stage coach' stopped to change horses and then continued with its journey with as little delay as possible. Without a change of horses a journey of any length was, inevitably, extremely slow.

The use of proper stages, with fresh horses for each stage, was another improvement first developed by the mail service and the increasing use of the mail coaches to carry passengers forced the stage coach companies to compete. The use of short, quick stages was greatly helped by improved road building techniques which made it a practical proposition to pull a coach more quickly, and as we have seen, coach construction was greatly improved also. With the frequent provision of a fresh team of horses the speed at which they were driven could be increased significantly. With the possibility of faster travel the demand for such journeys grew and so the short stage became an economic necessity for the coach companies. Soon the average length of a stage became eight to ten miles. Typical was the road to Brighton through Lewes where, from London, the first stage was ten miles, followed by stages of nine and ten miles, then a 13 mile stage crossing Ashdown Forest followed by two eight mile stages. With short routes and stricter timekeeping even the smaller companies found they could supply relays of horses and most journey times decreased dramatically.

The services provided by the inns themselves changed over the years. What had been a leisurely halt for a glass of beer and a chat with acquaintances along the way eventually became a time of frantic haste. Where passengers were allowed to purchase refreshment, they scarcely had time to swallow many mouthfuls before being hurried back into the coach and, where the stop was simply for a change of horses, the coach could pull up at an inn and the entire change of horses could be accomplished in less than one minute. Lord William Pitt Lennox commented on the dinners provided by coaching inns. When travelling in his own carriage, the meal provided was of good quality. When stopping as a stage coach passenger, however, he could be given scalding soup which was little more than stained water, tough steaks, underdone mutton and potatoes still hard inside. In fairness to the innkeepers, it must have been difficult to provide anything reasonable in the short time available even on scheduled refreshment stops, while private travellers were prepared to delay their journey appropriately. It has to be stated, however, that many of the inns on the Brighton roads had a fine reputation for good food.

Henry Hine, an outstanding coachman who had started his driving in the early years of the nineteenth century, was both coachman and coach owner on the Brighton road in 1831 and was obliged to travel faster in order to keep pace with his competitors. His attitude to the changes was probably typical of many of the older coachmen: "we don't travel half so comfortably now as we used to do. It is all hurry and bustle nowadays, sir – no time even for a pipe and a glass of grog." This comment is hardly surprising as Hine had started his driving in the very first years of the century with two-horse coaches and, at that time, four and a half miles per hour was considered a respectable pace. London to Brighton in 12 hours was quite all right.

Mail coaches had used stages of no more than ten miles for years before the shorter stage became generally used, but gradually the speed of the stage coaches improved and, by about 1825, their speed started to rival that of the mails. The recognised rate of driving for a stage coach was at a trot which maintained a speed on the Brighton road, including stops, of between six and seven miles per hour.

The overall time of journeys was much reduced when road improvements had advanced sufficiently to make it safe to travel at night. The poor nature of the earlier roads meant that night travel was too dangerous to be considered. Once coaches could travel after dark, overnight stops, particularly in the dark days of winter, could be made shorter and so time actually on the road increased.

Even on the comparatively short distance to Brighton, travel in darkness allowed an increase in the variety of journey times available, with either earlier starts or later arrivals.

In general on the Brighton road, daytime travel was preferred as being more convenient for passengers and also faster than at night. Of the 35 regular coach departures from London in 1817, 20 left between 8.00 and 9.30 in the morning for a six- or seven- hour journey. Seven left in the afternoon and would have arrived after dark in the winter months. The earliest and latest coaches, with one exception, were from the Golden Cross, Charing Cross, at six in the morning and three in the afternoon respectively. The exception was the night coach from the Blossom Inn, Cheapside, which left at 8.30 in the evening.

Lord William Pitt Lennox is quoted as saying

> "... when the Prince Regent... selected Brighton, as a marine residence... the journey from London to this small fishing town occupied two days; the first night being passed at Reigate or at Cuckfield, according to the road the stage travelled... it was not until 1823 that the Brighton road became... the first in England for well appointed coaches, first rate teams, and gentleman-like drivers."

The period of "well appointed coaches" and "first rate teams" was the Golden Age of coaching; the time when coach travel was at its height between 1824 and 1848.

Plate 6

The *Age* outside the Bull and Mouth Regent Circus, Piccadilly. This coach, once driven by Harry Stevenson, was one of the most famous on the Brighton road.

Plate 7

At the Elephant and Castle in 1826. A major crossroads for traffic in coaching times as well as today.

Plate 8

Kennington in 1842. A relaxing place, despite what was, for the time, a busy road.

Plate 9

Kennington Gate. The gate was notorious for delays and accidents. All the London to Brighton traffic had to pass through it.

Chapter 3
The Lewes Route: Streatham to Godstone

At Streatham the main coach route south was joined by another coach road, to the west of Streatham High Road, which provided a link through to the alternative, western, Brighton road, joining that road at Balham. This road could be used, if desired, as a different way into London for coaches travelling north from Croydon. The road is worth a passing comment due to a widely reported incident which involved the Prime Minister William Pitt, the Chancellor Lord Thurlow and Mr Dundas, Treasurer of the Navy. The road had a toll gate on Bedford Hill and the three eminent gentlemen rode past the gate. They were returning from a convivial evening with Mr Jenkinson at Addiscombe House. According to the *Bolton Chronicle* of September 3rd 1831, the Noble Lords, returning on horseback late on Saturday night:

> "Finding the Turnpike-Gate, situate between Tooting and Streatham, thrown open, and being elevated above their usual prudence, passed through the gate at a brisk pace without stopping to pay the toll, regardless of the remonstrances and threats of the turnpike man, who running after them, believing them to belong to some thieves who have recently committed depredations in the neighbourhood, discharged the contents of his blunderbus at their backs. Happily for them, he was no marksman. The mistake of the Turnpikeman was a very natural one from their conduct."

The account gives a delightfully human insight into the nature of both turnpike men and cabinet ministers in the coaching age. The very name *blunderbuss* seems so totally appropriate to the age in which it was in use. How very different from our own age, with its strict laws on gun ownership, was a time when it was thought quite reasonable for the turnpike man to have a blunderbuss and to use it! How very different also was a time when government ministers rode home on horseback, without any special security, and had ample leisure to ride out and get drunk with friends.

The main Brighton road leaves Streatham to the south where it crosses the River Graveney at Hermitage Bridge. This small river flows through an ugly concrete box today, a depressing example of twentieth-century functionalism. In coaching days it was a much more significant feature and, no doubt, much more attractive. The original bridge is said to have been built in 1652 by the Worshipful Company of Merchant Taylors after one of their members was nearly drowned, having been thrown from his horse while fording the stream.

A toll gate, known as Streatham Gate or Hermitage Gate, stood to the south of the bridge, and beyond it the road once more entered open country of woods and heath. Nowadays this is a mundane road of undistinguished buildings linking London, without interruption, to the built-up area of Croydon. In the past it was all peaceful countryside. Describing Norwood, just to the east of the Brighton road, Edwards wrote:

> "Norwood – The Horns, a very decent public house or inn, which is much frequented in the summer season by genteel people from London, and as this rural place bears no marks of its vicinity to the capital, those who are fond of occasional contemplation of unimproved Nature, will find great satisfaction in a visit to Norwood."

Not everyone spent their time in Norwood contemplating unimproved nature. The countryside thereabouts was a mixture of cultivated land, woodland and heath; not particularly prosperous as much of the soil was poor. Wild areas meant that there were haunts for thieves, for whom the contemplation of nature was certainly not a first consideration. One such wild area near Thornton Heath was a favourite haunt of highwaymen. As elsewhere, this was dealt with by hanging those who were caught. A large gallows was positioned near Thornton Heath pond, in an area otherwise known as Gallows Green. The original horse pond was later made into an ornamental area with a fountain playing. Now it has a small patch of grass, some paving and a few shrubs. When building work was carried out in later years a number of skeletons, believed to be of executed highwaymen, were dug up near the pond. As executions continued to happen at this place, it would seem that their deterrent value was limited, but they must surely have had some effect in reducing the number of robbers on the road. On August 13th 1720, a highwayman named John Sculthorp was hanged. On March 31st 1722 six men were hanged; in the next year, four more. Most of these were hanged for highway robbery. The sight of gallows and gibbets was presumably accepted as a normal part of the scenery on the roads out of London. A gallows was typically used for executions and a gibbet for exhibiting the corpse of the felon. Surely the road that passed by Gallows Green would have been avoided by persons of sensibility or with a weak stomach!

South of Thornton Heath the area of Broad Green was, as its name implies, a wide grassy area. All the greenery is now gone, with the exception of the name.

Over the last century Croydon has changed more than any other town on the Brighton roads. The reason is not just the result of urban sprawl, although Croydon has more miles of undistinguished housing than most places. It is not even the mini-skyscraper office blocks which, like any office blocks, lack the soul of a building that is also lived in. It is as if a succession of town councils and planning departments have come together in an unholy alliance to tear the heart out of the town. In much of the place the tendency seems to have been to destroy old buildings and replace them with something newer, more economically viable, functional, usually ugly and divorced from the past. As a result the town is almost unrecognisable when compared with illustrations done before 1900.

One of the few old buildings to have survived is the Hospital of the Holy Trinity of John Whitgift. This is a charming building, mercifully preserved from the depredations of Croydon's latter day developers. It provides an oasis of tranquillity and still performs its original function of giving a home to some of the elderly of Croydon. It also houses the offices of the Whitgift Foundation. This is one of the few buildings remaining in the town that a coach traveller would recognise were he to pass through Croydon today.

In the past, Croydon was a typical market town and a major stop for coaches from London. The town offered the choice of a number of inns where travellers could make their first change of horses. The first of these, situated at what was then the north end of the town, stood just opposite Whitgift Hospital. It was the Crown Inn, now remembered only in the name of Crown Hill, at the top of which it stood. The main Croydon shopping street today is North End but the Crown marked the beginning of the old heart of Croydon, south down the High Street. At one time a well-known landlord of the Crown was an ex-pugilist named Martin. He was a prize fighter who had also been a baker before taking up fighting and so was known as 'Master of the Rolls'. An inn sign extended across the width of the street to link the Crown with Whitgift Hospital.

Two other inns had their signs right across the street – 'gallows' signs, as they were often termed. These were the Greyhound in the High Street and the King's Arms in Katherine Street, the latter opening into the High Street. When wagons piled high with produce, particularly pockets of Sussex hops which reached to a great height, approached these signs they sometimes had to be stopped and unloaded before they could proceed further as the load was too high to pass under the sign.

The Greyhound was possibly the most famous of all the Croydon inns, and shared royal patronage with the King's Arms. The latter is famous for a story concerning George IV who is said to have changed horses at the King's Arms at the time when he was estranged from Queen Caroline. There was strong feeling in the town in favour of the queen and a lounger leaned through the window and enquired of the king, "Why didn't you bring the wife, George?" The king was so angry at this treatment that he refused ever to pass through Croydon thereafter. A little further south along the High Street, just south of Scarbrook Road, was another important posting inn, the Green Dragon. This, like the other inns, served some of the main London and Brighton coaches. Although the stables attached to the inn have long gone, the inn itself remains but is completely changed in structure from its appearance in coaching days. Instead of serving coaches, it now provides refreshment and entertainment for the stallholders and customers of Surrey Street market.

As Croydon was the first important staging post on the road to Brighton its inns flourished accordingly. Famous coaches to stop here included the *Sovereign*, the *Dart* and the *Old Times*. In addition, the Royal Mail changed horses daily at the Green Dragon at four in the morning and 9.45 in the evening. At any time of day, whichever of the inns a coach was accustomed to use would have been ready to supply a good meal. In the earlier days of coaching this would have been a reasonably leisurely affair but, as the nineteenth century advanced, the demands for an ever faster journey, even in a town as large as Croydon, where a longer stop may have been allowed, would have meant a frantically hurried meal if the passengers were not to be left behind.

Patterson's Roads, a standard road book for the users of turnpikes, informs us that Croydon was notable for other activities apart from its market and its coaching inns. It was a flourishing place for many types of field sports:

> "The vicinity of this town is particularly celebrated for field sports, and the chase here is kept up with great spirit, as will appear from the following packs of hounds which are kennelled in the neighbourhood, and are as follows:– Lord Derby's stag hounds at the Oaks at Woodmanstern, 4m from Carshalton; the Surrey subscription fox hounds, late Mr. Maberley's at Cold Harbour; Mr. Jolliffe's fox hounds, at Merstham, about 6m off; Mrs Gee's harriers, Beddington Park, 1 mile; and the Banstead and Sanderstead harriers."

Such activities would hardly be possible in the urbanised Croydon area of today but the interested observer may notice the number of public houses still to found in the Croydon area with names which have a connection with hunting, though none of the inns in the town itself had such a connection.

To an explorer of the coach roads Croydon is a sad town. Surely it would have been possible to preserve and maintain at least one of the old inns. How the town would be enhanced if it were still possible to have a drink in the Greyhound or the King's Arms! Modern inns often try to replicate the characteristics of a past age but present day contrivance can never reproduce the authenticity of the original, which seems to have soaked into and become part of its very fabric. An old print shows the Greyhound facing across the High Street where a wagon has stopped to make a delivery outside. The sign across the street has a picture of a greyhound depending from it, and above, within a wrought iron frame, a sign advertising post horses.

The Croydon inns were important for serving much other traffic as well as stage coaches. The nobility and gentry, even the king himself, would change horses here. They were posting inns, where horses were available for hire so that a fresh team could be harnessed to a gentleman's private carriage and his own tired horses stabled and attended to. Every town had one or more posting inns which could guarantee to provide fresh horses from their extensive stables. These were ridden by post boys employed by the inn, who controlled the horses on their journey to the next change and were responsible for bringing the horses back to their own stable. Individuals without a carriage could hire riding horses at a posting house, or hire a post chaise. Most post masters were innkeepers and to use the term 'posting inn' meant it had ample stabling and could be relied on to provide whatever type of transport was required.

The term *posting* had nothing to do with the post office; it was simply used to give an impression of speed. In appearance a post chaise looked like a coach with the front section removed. It could accommodate two or three passengers facing forwards and had room for their luggage. The chaise was normally drawn by two horses, or four if road conditions demanded it. The horses were driven by the post boy, or postillion, riding the nearside horse, and were usually driven at the gallop.

The post 'boys' were often elderly men who had formally been in service. They wore a distinctive uniform of a yellow jacket – or sometimes blue – in the south of England and a red jacket in the north. In addition they wore breeches, short top boots and a large fluffy beaver hat.

The post chaise itself, or 'yellow bounder', was often an old private chariot. It succeeded the 'diligence' which was the popular name for 'fast' coaches during the second half of the eighteenth century. Post coaches and light post coaches ranked just after post chaises for speed. They carried three or four inside passengers and one or two outsides with only a small amount of luggage.

The great attraction of 'travelling post' was that it was much faster than a stage coach and the customer did not have to share space with other passengers. However, the cost of posting was always considerably more than the cost of using public vehicles. In 1775 a traveller paid nine pence a mile to travel post from London to Croydon, in addition to the charge for horses. In 1827 Robert Smith and his wife paid two shillings a mile from London to Brighton by post chaise and, with extras for their expenses on the road, the journey cost them more than £20, a very large sum in those days.

Posting inns did not necessarily cater for stage coaches. In many towns private coaches and stage coaches were served at different inns, and the proprietors of posting inns would look down their noses at stage coach passengers. One unfortunate aspect of coaching inns, which is referred to by many writers, was the poor quality of food and service provided. When the guard sounded his horn as the coach approached an inn, the signal was intended to ensure that a change of horses was quickly available, and also that a meal should be served as soon as possible. Passengers would be ushered into a dining room but might be allowed as little as ten minutes for breakfast and 20 minutes for lunch. By the time they were served there may have been time for little more than a few mouthfuls. At some of the worst inns, service could be deliberately slow, or food such as soup served scalding hot, so that when the unfortunate passengers had, perforce, to rush back onto the coach to avoid being left behind, the food remained to be offered again to the next coach or even the one after that. Most of these comments were not directed against Brighton road establishments, but sometimes inns on these routes acquired a bad name and were avoided where possible.

Croydon is one of those dispiriting suburban towns which have no clear beginning or end. The urban sprawl south of Streatham becomes Croydon through a sort of seamless transition, and the many uninspiring buildings to the south have, with a few exceptions, the same weary characteristic.

In coaching times the buildings of Croydon came to an end just past the junction with Southbridge Road and north of the Swan and

Sugar Loaf. This was the site of the Croydon toll gate, and beyond it lay the open country. A map of 1800 shows the toll house as a small building in the middle of the road but this must have been rebuilt later, as a watercolour in the possession of Croydon Library shows it at the eastern side and with an imposing pillared porch. On the other side of the road is a stream, the Croydon Bourne, which started a permanent flow from ponds near Haling Park and flowed down Southbridge Road to pass the parish church, and was one of the principle sources of the River Wandle. In one incident recorded here in July 1799, three miles south of the gate two highwaymen held up a chaise driven by a Mr Eastcourt and robbed him of his money and his watch. When the robbers were out of sight, Mr Eastcourt and the post boy set off in pursuit. They nearly overtook their quarry at the gate and were joined by two farmers who helped in the chase. One of the robbers was finally caught at Streatham and the missing watch was recovered.

There is no River Wandle visible beside the Brighton road today, and only the name Southbridge Road hints at its former existence. The river can be seen no more in modern Croydon, but is confined to an underground culvert. The buildings of South Croydon continue beside the road, except where they are relieved by the green oasis which is the grounds of Whitgift School. Today's built-up roadside hides the change in landscape which, to coach travellers, was significant. Coaches passed through the Croydon toll gate and entered the chalk country. Chalk hills, covered with a mixture of downland pastures and patches of woodland, stretched ahead of the traveller for the next eight miles. In places where the slopes rose steeply, the white faces of chalk quarries were evidence of an important local industry. Just south of Croydon the chalk was cut back to leave a great white cliff 60 feet high at the Haling lime works. The lime produced from this 'white stone' was largely sent north to London, being in demand for use in building the ever-expanding city. For the coaches the chalk meant clouds of white dust in the summer but a good, firm, well-drained surface beneath the wheels. The last permanent flowing water had been left behind at the Wandle and none would be met again until the geology changed once more north of Godstone.

South from Croydon the traveller can still see a few overgrown faces of old chalk workings, much degraded now and certainly not the dominant features of coaching days. However, what is still left serves as a reminder that the coaches passed through a semi-industrialised landscape on this part of the Brighton road. Quarrying, both at Haling and further south at Merstham, was of great importance and the products were carried northwards by what was then a marvel of industrial modernity, the Surrey Iron Railway, which ran for some distance beside the coach road. The railway was originally built to carry goods between Wandsworth and Croydon but in 1805 was extended to Merstham and renamed the Croydon, Merstham and Godstone Iron Railway. Wagons were pulled by horses along rails which had flanges on their outer sides. The wagon wheels were not flanged, as with later railways, which made it possible for them to be pulled on normal roads if necessary. The railway continued in operation until 1838 when its track was purchased by the London and Brighton Railway and steam power made its services redundant. In its day, however, it was a successful innovation which enabled one horse to pull a load of five tons uphill to the south, and twice that down the slope to the north.

The long valley south of Croydon, which stretches to the present town of Coulsdon, is known as Smitham Bottom. Now, inevitably, it is a built-up road. For the coaches it was a long, lonely valley with very few buildings; just fields sloping gently down to the road on each side. The only feature of note was another gibbet. This stood on a piece of land known as Gibbet Green, situated on land behind the Red Deer public house. By 1844 this place had become much less lonely and daunting. The tithe map of that date shows an extensive area of "house, stabling, sheds, yards" here. It was probably the site of the Brighton Road stables, maintained by that leading coach company proprietor, William Chaplin.

There is now no remnant of the open countryside that once bordered the roadside here. Woodland shows amongst the houses up the hillside however, and the coach road also soon headed up onto the hills. The present road to Brighton continues along the easy gradients of Smitham Bottom through Coulsdon, and the Iron Railway continued on this route, but the original coach road climbed up onto the firm dry chalk, away from the soft surface and occasional Bourne floods through what is now Purley. The place where the old road turns off is up Riddlesdown Road from Purley Oaks, a long steady pull up a very ancient road. This is part of the Roman road, the London–Lewes Way, sections of which had survived in use through the centuries.

The Purley Oaks area is not attractive, but has improved from the condition that Harper described in 1892 as "a very disreputable and stony road... A derelict highway... Now ending obscurely in a miserable modern settlement near the newly built railway station of Purley Oaks". The road is no longer disreputable or stony, and the area improves once away from the valley floor. Eventually the tarmac ends and the road continues as a track along the crest of the chalk ridge of Riddlesdown. A comparison of the present landscape with a map from coaching days shows that here survives the first scrap of what could be called 'proper countryside': an area where the scene would not, perhaps, be too unfamiliar to the coach traveller of old. There are views of wooded hills in all directions and, although they are now dotted with houses, the scenery familiar to coach travellers can be easily envisaged. The coaches had now travelled sufficiently far from the influence of London for this to be the point on his journey to Brighton where the coachman would have palpably relaxed. The slow uphill grind since leaving London had been accomplished; the dangers of the wild heaths between London and Croydon had been passed, and for the many who intended to change horses at Godstone the end of the stage was approaching with its usual opportunity for rest and refreshment.

The slopes of Riddlesdown are much more wooded today than when they were extensively grazed sheep pastures, but the downland grasses and patches of woodland are still typical of the North Downs hills. The old road soon descends through the trees, however, as a sunken track which can only have resulted from the erosion of many centuries. It joins the present main road, the A22, opposite the site of the Rose and Crown public house. The old inn was of lath and plaster, and with some doors only five feet high. It was demolished in 1929 and now even its successor has been removed.

By the end of the eighteenth century road building techniques had advanced sufficiently for Riddlesdown to be bypassed by a road between the Red Deer and the Rose and Crown. Patterson's guide of 1808 says "By keeping along Smitham Bottom to the right about half a mile and bearing left a new road is made to the Rose and Crown inn which avoids Riddlesdown Hill." This runs to the present Purley crossroads and then becomes the main A22 road of today. After Purley it follows a wide terrace cut into the steep hillside above the potentially wet land of the valley bottom. It must have been a significant feat of engineering to construct such a road at that time, and it is one of the earliest examples of a new low-level road replacing one of the high chalk tracks.

When the new road was completed the milestones were removed from Riddlesdown and repositioned. Two of them may still be seen. One is in the grounds of Purley Hospital; the other by the roadside about 150 yards north of the Rose and Crown. Both are fine, square stones of limestone and give the distances to London. The Purley stone says "XII Miles from Westminster Bridge XIII miles from the Standard in Cornhill 1743". Being made of limestone it is now much weathered, and not all the lettering can be made out. The stone north of the Rose and Crown is one mile further from London and partly obscured by a concrete base built to protect it.

The erection of these milestones was referred to in the *London Evening Post* of 10th September 1743:

> "On Wednesday they began to measure the Croydon Road from the Standard in Cornhill and stake places for erecting milestones, the inhabitants of Croydon having subscribed for thirteen which tis hoped will be carried on by the gentlemen of Sussex."

The distance to Cornhill was, of course, by the London Bridge route. The distance to Westminster, also shown on the milestones, was in anticipation of a route not yet in existence, as Westminster Bridge was not opened until November 10th 1750.

This section of road connects the built-up areas of Purley (known in coaching days as Foxley Hatch) and Kenley and, apart from looking at the milestones, it is worth visiting an area of grass in Purley known as the Rectory Field. A terrace of grass across the field marks the route of the Iron Railway and at one side of the field a short section of the original flanged track has been preserved.

The road continues through the present nondescript settlement of Whyteleafe and arrives at the large Wapses Lodge roundabout, where roads to the left lead to Woldingham and Warlingham and on the right to Caterham. The road here is built up above the level of the surrounding land, which is screened by bushes and trees. Tucked down within a corner between two of the roads that meet here is a small building which appears to be a toll house. It has a typical toll house design with brick and weatherboarding and a porch projecting from the front, with windows on each side through which the toll keeper could see coaches approaching. Stage coaches expected no delay when the guard sounded the 'yard of tin' to signify their approach. Mail coaches were in even more of a hurry and expected the gates to be open for them to sweep through without stopping, as they were exempt from the toll. This house is in the right position to collect tolls from vehicles entering from the side roads that meet here but, unlike all the other Brighton road toll houses, it does not appear on any map of the period. It could be a fine remnant of the coaching age but is probably not what it appears, and is destined to remain an enigma.

There used to be an inn serving coaches just south of Wapses Lodge on the site which is now a centre for car sales. This inn was for sale by auction on 9th July 1833 and the auction particulars give a good idea of the size of an average establishment supplying horses on a busy road, although it was not a stop for stage coaches.

> "A well-accustomed inn, known by the sign of The Half Moon, situate in Stonham Lane, on the Turnpike Road from Croydon to Godstone, with convenient Offices, Yards, and Gardens; Stables for fifty horses, with Loose boxes; Coach-house, Granary; and other out-buildings; and Nine Acres, Two Roods, and Twenty-Four Perches of Freehold Land..."

The rent for this extensive property was £56.18s a year. Here we have more detail to emphasise the tremendous importance of horses and stabling along the coach roads. There were no other buildings in the Caterham valley until the coming of the railway, and the village was up on the hill above. The coach road passed between fields, but here was a thriving business depending entirely upon the traffic passing along the road. The Half Moon was the exact parallel of an isolated petrol station found beside a main road through the country today, except for the land attached to it which presumably helped provide for the horses.

Up through Caterham Valley, a settlement which owes its existence to the railway and so postdates the coaching age, the turnpike road passed through fields all the way with no buildings at all until the outskirts of Godstone were reached. The road climbs gently through one of the easiest passages through the North Downs, the dry gap above Godstone. Views of the Wealden hills open up before travellers as they come through the gap. James Hassel, writing about the Godstone Gap in 1817, says:

> "The country about this spot assumes a novel appearance, the hills being remarkably sharp and abrupt; rise immediately from the sides of the road, which, all the way from Godstone, lies between hills and abounds in chalk, and stiff clay on either side of which are hedges and brush underwood."

Only part of the present road follows the original coach road. It leaves the line of the present road from a layby on the eastern side and follows a track which is on the line of the old Roman road, rejoining the present road further down the hill. A cutting has been made to reduce the gradient at the top of the hill, and elsewhere the track is considerably sunken by natural erosion of the slope. It is a strange trackway, giving the passer-by the feeling that there is something wrong here. Trees grow thickly and overshadow the track, giving the illusion that it is a long way from any habitation. Perhaps it was more open in coaching times but, as it is now, it feels as if coach passengers would have expected to see a highwayman behind every bush, and passage at night would have been frightening. The old track was replaced with a new road, on the line of the present A22, in about 1850, and a milestone from the old road was repositioned. It can still be seen beside the modern road; another stone of the 1743 series, XIX miles from the Standard in Cornhill.

From this point on, the chalk country is left behind and the road descends to the clays and sands of the Weald. The traveller now enters a more intimate countryside, where woods, streams and fields constantly reveal new vistas of rich farmland and red brick houses.

Brick is not the only local building material, however. Oak from the woodlands, remnants of the old Wealden forest, is used everywhere and, in the Godstone area, another important building material was produced. Outcropping at the base of the chalk hills and dipping gently beneath them was a coarse stratum of the Upper Greensand formation known as hearthstone. The hills in this area contain miles of tunnels from which the hearthstone was removed. It was formerly in demand for many commercial purposes. Many of the old hearthstone tunnels have now collapsed but others remain, penetrating quite a long way under the ground. A major reason for maintaining the turnpike road was the large amounts of sand and hearthstone that had to be transported along it.

Coaches would have passed cartloads of stone being pulled slowly towards London. They would then have passed through the appropriately named Quarry House Gate, which is shown on the tithe map of 1840 to have been an isolated building amongst the fields. No sign of any toll house has survived here, but another milestone stands at the A25 junction. This time it is XX miles to the Standard in Cornhill, and the date is 1744. Presumably the task of making and erecting the milestones had taken some time, as they were started the previous year. This seems to be the only one of the five remaining milestones of the series to have survived in its original position. Soon after the milestone is Godstone Green. The White Hart, which looks across the green and its attractive pond, was familiar to all passengers on this road and a favourite stopping place for coaches. Unlike some of the inns further north, here is a fine survivor of the coaching age, still well able to care for a passing traveller.

Plate 10

Croydon High Street in 1830, looking north from the Green Dragon. A horse can be seen going down Scarbrook Road to the stables behind the inn.

Plate 11

View from the Green Dragon today. Buildings between Surrey Street and the High Street are on the same sites as in 1830. The eastern side of the High Street was moved back when the road was widened by 21 feet in 1896.

Plate 12

A milestone of the 1743–44 series. This one at Godstone is the only one to have remained in its original position.

Plate 13

The White Hart at Godstone. A stopping place for many coaches and many famous people. The nearby pond was typical of those found beside inns. They were valuable watering places for horses and farm animals on the road.

Chapter 4
The Lewes Route: Godstone to Lewes

The turnpike road ran beside Godstone Green and its pond, both of which can still be seen. It is a delightful sight on a summer's day, quintessentially English, when the White Hart looks across to a game of cricket and ducks paddle around on the pond. The coach house of the inn is still there too, now converted into a restaurant.

Many famous people must have stopped at the White Hart and probably the most prominent of these were the Prince Regent, when Prince of Wales, and the Czar of Russia who stayed there before going to witness a prize fight at nearby Blindley Heath. This heath was but one of the various prize-fighting venues along the Brighton roads. Places like Blindley Heath were chosen as they were large enough to accommodate the many carriages of the sporting fraternity who turned out to witness the spectacle. They were also within reach of London, but at a sufficiently discrete distance to avoid unwelcome interference with the proceedings. Other venues for prize fights were Crawley Down and Copthall Common where, in 1810, a famous fight took place between the champion of England, Tom Crib and Molineaux the Black.

Godstone pond is one of many found along all the main roads. They were of great importance for watering animals, but they were of particular importance near coach houses as a regular supply of water was needed for the horses and the coaches themselves could be left to stand in the water when necessary, to swell the wood of the wheels and so tighten old, loose joints.

The road south from Godstone epitomises the nature of the countryside between the chalk ridges of the North and South Downs. This area, still well wooded as befits the former Wealden forest, was apparently designed by nature to make cross-country travel difficult, with its steep-sided valleys cutting through damp clay and loose sandy ridges. The original road south of Godstone followed the Roman route over Tilburstow Hill. It was still the main road on Cary's map of 1810. Gradients were a problem but were eased by a deep cutting at the crest of the hill, a cutting which is very obvious on the modern road. Now, as in the past, much of this road is through woodland. Some of the traffic may have been visiting Iron Pear Tree House. This still stands on the southern slope of the hill and used to be famous for the provision of water from its well. This water was sold in specially produced bottles and, at one time, supplies were sent daily to the White Hart. It was claimed to be an efficacious remedy for gout.

On this road coaches would first encounter one of the many sandy ridges that lie across the Weald of Surrey and Sussex. The sand is loose and crumbly which meant that here, and throughout the sandstone areas, it was very difficult to maintain a firm surface. As with other fine sands found on the approaches to London, roads across the sandstone ridges in Surrey and Sussex could readily degenerate into a sea of dry dust during a summer drought. Narrow iron-tyred wheels quickly dug deep ruts into the sandy soil and the sandstone itself was ground into a powder. Heavy goods wagons did the greatest harm, particularly, as was a common practice, where the tyres were fitted with iron bolt heads which protruded about an inch from the tyre to give greater purchase on steep ground. These bolts tore up a solid surface and dug deep where it was soft. An act of 1763 attempted to outlaw vehicles where the wheels were less than nine inches wide at the rim. The hope was that wide wheels would act like rollers and consolidate the ground. Some were made with wheels as wide as 16 inches, but the legislation was largely ignored and then repealed. Wide wheels were unpopular as the extra friction made them difficult to pull and they lacked manoeuvrability. They did not even improve the surface as their weight broke up the weak sandstone and so increased the area of powdered sand.

South of Tilburstow Hill there is no alternative but to travel across the clay. The difficult sandy slopes were left behind and the lower-lying (and even more difficult) clay lands were entered. However, once road building techniques improved, the lower gradients of the clay lands provided an easier passage than the sandstone ridge and, as with other roads over the hills, the Tilburstow Hill route was eventually replaced by a new road at a lower level. This is the present A22, which was probably built soon after 1810, and when walking along it, it is immediately apparent that the construction would have presented great engineering problems. Where the new road branches off the old route it is built up on high banks above the very marshy woodland, which is inadequately drained by Gibbs Brook. Down the bank the woodland floor is still damp and spongy on a dry summer's day. Clearly such land would have been impossible for wheeled traffic, and similar damp valley bottoms are crossed many times before the chalk of the South Downs is reached. The problem has been solved at Godstone by raising the road on its high bank, and a similar technique was used on most other roads on the way to Brighton.

The frequent streams crossed on the road south from Godstone form the upper waters of the River Medway, many first finding their way into the Eden. They have all cut deeply into the countryside but as the embankments are now covered with trees and bushes they are not obvious to motorists on the modern road. They are much more obvious to the traveller on foot, and to the coachman of old they were only too real. These steep-sided, damp-bottomed ghylls are found throughout the Weald and are frequently crossed in the low-lying land south of Godstone. Their wooded slopes are linear remnants of the great forest that once filled the space between the North and South Downs with a sea of green. The ancient wildwood has long gone but, without any practical use other than as a source of fence posts and firewood, these narrow valleys have remained as woodland through the centuries. While the fields beside them are tended, many miles of ghylls are seldom penetrated. It is likely that, before the roads were properly engineered, the streams and the steep-sided valleys, rather than the milestones, were the most significant markers of the coachman's journey. Time and again the coach must have had to lurch down the steep slope of a ghyll, ford a stream bed and be heaved up the slope on the opposite side. No wonder they were avoided where possible, and modern roads are engineered to be well above them.

At this point it is relevant to consider further the extreme importance of the underlying geology to the roads south from London to the sea. The low-lying landscape which stretched south of Godstone owes its existence to the Weald Clay. A great semicircle of Weald Clay, the Low Weald, stretches around the sandstone core of south-east England, the High Weald, and the roads to Brighton have to cross both its northern and southern limbs. The widest of these clay areas lies in Surrey, but the clay of

Sussex had the worst reputation. Lying in a broad band across the county, the clay is crossed by the lower courses of the rivers Adur and Ouse. These waters, and the many small streams that flow into them, keep the land moist. In winter the roads of these regions were usually impassable until the improvements that took place during the second half of the eighteenth century. It may have been partly due to lack of custom, but it was mainly due to the state of the roads that coach services in the mid-eighteenth century did not operate in the winter. Even when roads improved it was many years before winter travel would be considered by most people unless a journey was absolutely essential. As late as the 1840s, when the macadamised roads of the turnpike trusts had transformed the state of the main routes, a minor road, like the lane between Staplefield and Slaugham, could still be marked on maps as "the summer road to Slaugham".

Such names as Slough Green and Slaugham speak for themselves about the nature of the land, and the writings of travellers abound with references to the miry nature of Sussex roads. In 1751 Dr Burton, in an oft-quoted account, wrote:

> "Why is it that the oxen, the swine, the women and all other animals are so long-legged in Sussex? May it be from the difficulty of pulling the feet out of so much mud by the strength of the ankle, that the muscles get stretched, as it were, and the bones lengthened?"

Daniel Defoe, in his *A Tour of Britain*, written in 1724, describes Sussex roads as being so bad that it could take up to 22 oxen to haul a tree through the quagmire, and says that sometimes the roads could get so bad over the winter that the whole length of the summer was scarcely enough to allow them to dry out. He also refers to an observation he made near Lewes where "an ancient lady, and a lady of very good quality I assure you, drawn to church in her coach with six oxen, nor was it done in frolic or humour, but mere necessity, the way being so stiff and deep, that no horses could go in it". In the early days of coaching even regular stage coaches sometimes turned to the extra pulling power of oxen which, due to their splayed feet, were able to keep going over ground where a horse would become bogged down. One commentator reported that the Shoreham to London coach "frequently made use of a pair of oxen to drag it over some of the worst stretches of the road".

With roads like this there was little the traveller could do but grin and bear it. Not for nothing do the words *travel* and *travail* stem from the same root. An old Sussex story tells, with rather ponderous humour, how a gentleman saw a man's hat in the road and took a kick at it only to find the wearer's head underneath. The man said, "Here, that's my hat! Help me out, I'm stuck in a quagmire!" On being pulled out it was discovered that the man was on horseback! Other versions of the tale have the horse standing on a load of hay, which is even deeper in the mire and in turn being pulled by a team of horses.

In some places bands of limestone are to be found, and where this was the case the stone could be used to make a more durable surface. Elsewhere in the High Weald better roads could be made using cinder and slag from the old iron industry. On the clay of the Low Weald little was available apart from brushwood. This was used extensively but soon disappeared into the 'bottomless clay', wherein any road materials seemed to sink forever.

The only rock type which provided a reasonably firm and well-drained surface was the chalk. On the early maps there is a considerable contrast between the few roads on the clay lands and the many tracks criss-crossing the chalk hills. The chalk roads were so much better than others that routes approaching the Downs ran on to the chalk as soon as possible, despite the steep slopes that were bound to be encountered, and avoided the damp valley bottoms where gentle gradients were no compensation for the extra miles over the clay. Good examples of this are the hard pull up Beeding Hill which avoids the damp land of the Adur valley, and the road to Pycombe which was reached by way of Clayton Hill instead of the much easier gradient from Poynings, where the clay of the Vale of Newtimber was particularly wet and sticky.

Despite its former bad reputation for road travellers, all parts of the Low Weald are pleasant country, but to appreciate its pleasantness it is necessary to make short excursions off the modern road. There are woodlands with ancient oaks wonderfully carpeted with bluebells in the spring, meadows with cattle thigh-deep in lush grass and fields of wheat growing strongly in the heavy but fertile soil. In contrast the modern road is heavy with the noise and smell of traffic. Away from the road it is all too easy to think of coaching days as a perfect age, with horses and coaches fitting easily into a countryside of which they were an integral part. In fact, thanks in part to the problems presented by the underlying geology, it was an age of hard toil where farmers made a meagre living and coach travel across the Weald was frequently a penance.

As the road rises from the damp Gibbs Brook valley, another series of milestones starts. These are made of sandstone and are inscribed only on the side facing the road, rather than to north and south, with the distances given from Cornhill, in this case 22 miles. Four of these milestones remain, and the Arabic numbers would surely have been easier to read from a passing coach than the Roman numbers of the first series. Unlike the first series there is no distance given to Westminster Bridge. The 23 mile stone is still in place but difficult to see as it is buried up to its top in the road embankment. The 24 mile stone stands to the south of the junction of the old and new roads. This milestone marks the start of Blindley Heath, the site of the pugilistic contest already referred to. After the heath is the Blue Anchor public house, which is by the site of the Blue Anchor turnpike gate. The 25 mile stone, last of the sandstone series, stands on the opposite side of the road. The Blue Anchor itself has nothing remaining from the coaching age.

The Blue Anchor or Blindley Heath gate was four miles south of Godstone Green, well into the land of lush wet fields and marshy stream bottoms. The road avoiding Tilburstow Hill crosses four streams, including Gibbs Brook which is at least six feet wide. From the Blue Anchor gate to the foot of Woodcock Hill another five streams are crossed, two of them six feet wide with a powerful flow, and the largest, Eden Brook, is ten feet wide. There is much woodland amongst the fields here, and it is fairly safe to assume that this must always have been so because the carpets of bluebells seen here in the in spring are good indicators of ancient woodland.

There is a choice of two routes to Brighton from Newchapel, where a road turns off to the right beside a large pond. This road is followed in a later chapter. The main road south crosses the Eden Brook and then ascends the long slope of Woodcock Hill, rising up past the Woodcock Inn. There is a subtle change in the landscape here, due again to a change in geology. This is not yet the true High Weald but the underlying rock is now sandstone. For many miles from now on the coachmen would have had to face an uphill pull on sandy tracks.

Where the road again drops down to a valley at Felbridge there is an example of a very deeply incised ghyll, crossed now on a high bridge and embankment leaving the stream a long way below road level, and after this another long hill carries the road up into East Grinstead. Houses now extend down this road from the town centre but coaching memories are revived by the first of the Bow Bells mileposts, 29 miles from London, and still to be seen on the right hand side of the London Road, approaching East Grinstead. There used to be at least two others further north but they have been removed due to modern roadworks. From this point on, however, there stands a splendid series of small white posts, each with a cast iron plate depicting five bells of decreasing size surmounted by a bow, and by numerals which give the number of miles to London. Most measurements from London were from the Standard in Cornhill, or from the London Stone in Canon Street. The Bow Bells mileposts, however, give the distance from the church door of St. Mary-le-Bow. It has been suggested that these mileposts were set up on the instructions of Thomas Pelham-Holles, the Duke of Newcastle, when he was Prime Minister so that he could note his progress between 10 Downing Street and his great house at Halland Park; however this is disputed. It may be true on the road to Halland Park where the bow is surmounted by a buckle, the symbol of the Pelham family, but the buckle is absent on the mileposts along the Brighton road. The mileposts are carefully preserved and one, number 47, was recast as a replacement in 1957.

East Grinstead has a strong claim to be the first coaching town of any on the roads to Brighton, for it was the home of James Batchelar who, in May 1756, started the first coach service from London to Brighton. The family already ran coaches between London and East Grinstead and through to Lewes, but until 1756 the only way to continue beyond Lewes had been by private carriage or by carriers wagon.

An advertisement formerly on display at the Brighton Art Gallery and Museum says:

LEWES
and
Brighthelmftone
New Machine
To hold four Paffengers,

By Chailey,
Sets out from the George Inn in the Hay Market, St Jame's, at Six o'Clock in the Morning, every Monday, Wednesday and Friday, in one Day, to the Star at Lewes, and the Old Ship at Brighthelmftone, and returns from thence every Tuesday, Thurfday and Saturday. Infide paffengers to Lewes to pay Thirteen Shillings, to Brighthelmftone Sixteen Shillings; to be allowed Fourteen Pounds Weight of Luggage, all above to pay One Penny per Pound: Children in Lap and outfide pay Half Price: Half of the Fare to be Paid at Booking Perform'd [if God permit] by

J. BATCHELAR

N.B. Batchelar's old Godstone, Eaft Grinstead and Lewes Stage continues to fet
out every Tuesday at Nine o'Clock, and Saturday at Five o'Clock from the Talbot
Inn in the Borough

This was simply an extension of the existing London to Lewes service and was established 14 years before the road beyond Lewes was turnpiked. If, perhaps, the operation was a gamble to start with, it must have been a successful one as a rival service was soon being operated. Tubb and Brawne ran their "new Flying Machine" via Uckfield in 1762 and promised to complete the journey from London to Brighthelmstone in one day, returning the next. Horses were changed at Croydon, Godstone, East Grinstead, Uckfield and Lewes. The inside passengers were charged 13 shillings to Lewes and a further 3 shillings if continuing to Brighton. Outside passengers were conveyed for half the price. When Batchelar died in 1766 Tubb took over his business and, in partnership with Davis, ran coaches to Brighton on other routes also.

There remains in East Grinstead a Bow Bells milepost, number 30, just before the road bends sharply to the east. There are old buildings in the town which would have been familiar to coach travellers and the most important of these by far is the Dorset Arms. The Batchelar family owned the inn and lived there for many years. It was a major coaching inn with changes of horses for stage coaches and private vehicles. Some of the buildings behind the present inn were originally stables. Much has been altered inside but the frontage has been preserved.

The Dorset Arms was famous for its good luncheons and many notable people stopped at the inn on their way to Brighton. Spencer Percival, the Prime Minister who was later assassinated, liked to stay there. Another guest was Perdita Robinson, an actress and society beauty who would stay en route to Brighton and the bed of the Prince Regent. Unfortunately she never paid her bills at the Dorset Arms and eventually they had to be settled for her by the state.

The Prince Regent later transferred his favours to Mrs Fitzherbert, who must also have been familiar with the coach road and the attractions of the Dorset Arms. This was another lady of expensive tastes. Her 'turnout' – that is, her carriages and horses – was said to be "faultless" and her postillions "pictures". Like the media personalities of today she appears to have had plenty of money at her disposal, or perhaps, with the friendship of the Regent behind her, she was allowed plenty of credit.

East Grinstead was the next stop after Godstone for all coaches on the Lewes route. The earliest coach would have arrived by about 11 in the morning, three hours after leaving London, an important stop for refreshment and another change of horses. No doubt the coachman would have been very particular about the horses for the next stage of his journey as it involved some very difficult stretches of road and some of the most remote country on the route.

On leaving the town the coaches would pass through the East Grinstead toll gate. This was adjacent to the town gaol which survives today as a cottage with a small barred window looking across the road. Two tickets issued at this gate are preserved in the East Grinstead Museum. They are dated from the mid-eighteenth century; one is for sixpence and one for a shilling, not an insignificant amount for those days.

After the gate the old coach road followed a much more awkward route from the town than does the modern road. It remains as a short, sunken lane named Old Road, with cliffs of sandstone beside it lying to the north of the present road, an attractive little road which is as different from its successor as it could possibly be. Coachmen, however, hated it as it was steep and difficult to negotiate.

The road from East Grinstead to Forest Row, and even more so the continuation up to Wych Cross, seems to go on for a very long time. For coach travellers it must have felt like penetrating a wilderness. After the bustle of London and the lively activity of towns and villages all the way to East Grinstead the land of the High Weald must have seemed remote indeed. For the modern motorist the road can be simply a long crawl behind heavy lorries.

South of East Grinstead it is a long pull up to the first of the sandstone ridges of Ashdown Forest. There are houses scattered along the road now, but much woodland too, and old boundary banks run parallel to the road in many places. The present main road with its wide bends was constructed to avoid the steeper gradients of the old road through Ashurst Wood. The houses of Ashurst Wood lie along the old road and ignore the new road which, in turn, ignores them. Further Bow Bells mile posts stand all along this road which eventually descends to cross the Medway, two branches of which are here flowing strongly to the east. At Forest Row, then called Highgate, a Bow Bells mile post can be seen outside the post office. Another hill leads up into Ashdown Forest proper and passes further mile posts before reaching Wych Cross. Near here are two 35 mile Bow Bells posts. These date from the time when the road was altered to avoid Tilburstow Hill, a change which had the effect of adding just over half a mile to the length of the journey. The Wych Cross to Lewes trustees refused to move their mile post and so the Godstone to Highgate trustees had to add an extra post to theirs. The new post has an anthemion design instead of bells.

The road up to Wych Cross is often infested with slow-moving traffic. Less smelly, but even more slow-moving, the coaches of old struggled up the same hills. Various embankments and cuttings beside the road are evidence of alterations made to the hill for the benefit of coaches. In a number of places it is easy to see the tracks of past versions of the road, sometimes as broad ditches amongst the trees and elsewhere as a terrace-way above the level of the present road. Wych Cross is a small place, but represents an important parting of the ways where coaches could choose, as can modern traffic, whether to travel to Lewes by way of Uckfield or Chailey. The two roads were turnpiked in 1752 and a toll house was built in the fork between them. This survived until 1965 when it was demolished, but a milestone in the form of a large sandstone panel has been preserved at the site, mounted in a brick surround. This stone gives distances to Maresfield and Uckfield. There is no record of a similar stone for the Chailey route, but surely such a stone must have existed at one time. London to Brighton via Chailey was 57 miles; via Uckfield the journey was two miles longer.

The Act of 1752 was:

> "An Act for repairing the roads from the north end of Malling Street, near the town of Lewes, to Witch Cross, and from the north end of Malling Street aforesaid to the Broil Park Gate, and from Offham to Witch Cross aforesaid, all lying within the county of Sussex."

The roads are described as:

> "... in so bad a condition that they were impossible for wheeled carriages in winter, and very difficult and dangerous for persons travelling on horseback."

Reading this description of the road it is clear that the early coach proprietors, using these roads before many improvements had been undertaken, were brave as well as enterprising. Profits must have been anything but certain. The normal toll was one shilling for every four-wheeled carriage. The toll in winter for any carriage laden with chalk or timber was raised to two shillings and sixpence. Such heavy transport damaged the road and had to be made to pay for it.

Although the turnpiking of both alternatives occurred in 1752 the Uckfield road became the more frequented of the two, probably because of the extra trade generated by Uckfield itself. This road is measured by Bow Bells mileposts all the way to Lewes – not the case on the Chailey road.

In Ashdown Forest, as with the Low Weald on the clay, it is worth exploring the land around the road as well as the road itself. This shows, much more clearly than the modern road, the type of land the coachman would have had to deal with. His problems in Ashdown Forest were obvious. Steep tracks, treacherous with sand and loose stones, lead down the sides of the valleys, and they are often made worse where the rain has washed away gullies. Coaches would have swayed down such slopes with great difficulty and could then have quite possibly become bogged down in unexpected marshy areas where streams meander on the damp valley floor. Where they are not creating a marsh the streams are quite likely to be flowing in a ravine some four to six feet deep. There are plenty of streams because the forest is astride the watershed of the Ouse and Medway basins. To avoid the steepest of the valleys the road keeps to the highest land, above the sources of as many streams as possible. It is wild and open country, the haunt of many birds and with wonderful views of nearby woods and distant hills. Yet, despite the beauty of the area, it is easy to understand how it would have been disliked in the past. Much of the land is too poor to farm and so has been left as heathland. It would have been seen as an area over which it would have been hard to travel, and which would give little of value apart from firewood and poor pasture. William Cobbet, who crossed Ashdown Forest in 1830, would have found many in agreement with his verdict: "verily the most villainously ugly spot I ever saw in England". In contrast, Ashdown Forest is now much enjoyed by walkers, horse riders and picnicking families. On a summer's day visitors can buy an ice cream from a van at the roadside. What on earth would Cobbet have made of it all?!

The first part of the Uckfield route is the road from Wych Cross to Nutley, where the Shelley Arms was a coaching inn. This road traverses some of the highest and wildest parts of Ashdown Forest, and then gradually descends to a broad stream, one of the many Medway headwaters and one which could not be avoided. The steep slope down to this stream and the climb back up again would have been particularly difficult for coaches. The present road crosses the valley on an embankment some 20 feet high. This embankment, or at least the lower part of it, probably dates from the 1830s when many improvements were made to this part of the road including straightening the section between Nutley and Maresfield.

 Deep ghylls are again a feature of the road here. There is a particularly deep valley just north of Maresfield. Here the road has entered the basin of the River Ouse and so the river flows to the west. The road winds its way through the village, down the hill in a deeply eroded cutting, and crosses another stream before the site of the next toll gate is reached at Ringles Cross. This gate stood beside farm buildings just south of the junction of the A22 and A26 roads.

 The River Uck, about 15 feet wide, is a powerful tributary of the Ouse. Uckfield lies on its north side where the land slopes gently down to the river. Although the town was never of major importance to coaches from Brighton, the Maiden's Head was a well-known coaching inn. A directory of 1840 describes the accommodation at the Maiden's Head as "superior to what might be anticipated from the size and consequence of the village". The inn still stands today but sadly it has been much altered internally since coaching times.

After leaving Uckfield the road rises and falls gently across another seven miles of the Low Weald. It passes through a peaceful, well-watered, fertile landscape across which distances continue to be marked by Bow Bells mileposts. Once again valleys have been filled with embankments and so it is not obvious today how much more undulating the road used to be. Five significant streams are crossed, and in every case the road level is now well above them. There is an attractive church and green at Little Horsted and some of the fine old oak trees beside this part of the road are certainly old enough to have cast their shade over passing coaches.

The line of the South Downs now lies across the route ahead with a steady uphill section at Malling Hill before the coaches entered the chalky environs of Lewes. At last they were approaching the final lap of the journey, and the passengers would be alert for the sight and smell of the sea. A small row of cottages now stand beside the position of Malling Gate, the toll gate before Lewes, and unexpectedly, two different features of the old road suddenly appear. The first is two sections of the old coach road which remain as a track amongst the hedgerows, first on one side of the road and then on the other. Here also is the last Bow Bells milepost. The second is the old toll house itself. It used to stand in isolation but is now amongst other cottages, a typical rectangular toll house with the central part jutting forward to give a good view up and down the road. It looks a bit sad now, battered as it is by the noise and fumes of modern traffic and by objects thrown up by passing vehicles; however it is good to see that the toll house has survived; a fairly insignificant little building now, yet anything but insignificant when all the traffic on a busy road had to pass through its gate and pay for the privilege.

In December 1834 this toll gate was mentioned in the *Times*:

> "On Tuesday week a commercial gentleman left the White Hart Inn, Lewes, with a young man, a resident of Brighton (but a

perfect stranger to him) in his travelling gig, for Hastings. On arriving at Malling Hill, the gentleman had occasion to get out, and he gave the reins to his companion. The commercial traveller had scarcely turned his back, when he heard the horses feet going. He turned round, thinking there was some joke, but, to his great astonishment, he found the young man driving off with great rapidity, and in a short time the gig was out of sight. The traveller… made his way to the Malling- gate, on the London-road, and through this gate he found the gig had passed at a slapping pace. The gig, which contained money to a considerable amount and several boxes, has not been heard of."

The commercial traveller concerned seems to have been a fool! How many drivers today, driving a car loaded with valuables, would leave a perfect stranger in the driving seat and the key in the ignition? However, perhaps honesty was more readily assumed in those days. After passing the toll house the road soon crosses the top of Malling Hill and then curves steeply down to cross the Ouse at Lewes. Walking down Malling Hill on a fine day, it is hard to imagine this same road as it was on 8th January 1789. The road went through open country then and was very exposed to the elements. We hear a lot today about climate change and, despite global warming, we still get plenty of snow and icy roads. However, as far as snow is concerned, few modern winters can match those encountered by the coaches of old. Some snowstorms were of such severity that records have survived and become part of the history of the Brighton roads. The road from Malling Gate to Lewes suffered badly in 1789. It was blocked to such a depth of snow that it became almost indistinguishable from the surrounding countryside. The London coach could only avoid the great drifts by 'breaking the road' – that is, leaving the road and continuing its journey across country. The struggle for coachmen and horses alike must have been titanic and one can but admire the fortitude of travellers under such conditions. Modern drivers need fortitude of a different, but surely less demanding, kind when they are stuck in a traffic jam. Unfortunately for them, the possibility of 'breaking the road' is no longer an option. In that hard winter of 1789 further heavy snow fell continuously from the end of January through the first week of February. Heroic efforts were made to force a passage for the mails under such conditions, but otherwise the little traffic that had intended to move in the winter months stayed sensibly at home.

Plate 14

The Dorset Arms, East Grinstead. A famous coaching inn visited by the Prime Minister Spencer Percival, and by the Prince Regent with his mistress Perdita Robinson.

Plate 15

East Grinstead toll gate stood on the eastern edge of the town. Such gates were a familiar sight on all turnpike roads.

Plate 16

A Bow Bells milepost; one of the series marking the miles from St. Mary-le-Bow. Most survive from East Grinstead to Ashdown Forest and beyond.

Chapter 5

The Lewes Route: Wych Cross to Brighton through Chailey

The alternative road to Lewes takes the right hand fork at Wych Cross. This road too crosses some of the high, sandy land of Ashdown Forest, but it meets pockets of cultivation sooner than the alternative route and quickly leaves the high ridges behind. Like the Uckfield road it passes through the Ouse basin but to the western side of the main stream, so the tributaries flow east, and many of them are even more deeply incised than on the Uckfield route. Similarities with the Uckfield road remain to the end as coaches had to climb the chalk whichever way they went, in this case at Offham Hill, which has to be ascended before entering Lewes.

About four miles after leaving Wych Cross is the pleasant village of Danehill. Situated on a hill as its name suggests, it has attractive old buildings but the original road was bypassed in 1818 and the main road now lies to the east of the church, ignoring the hill on which it stands, and over which the old road climbed. Beyond the village are wide grass verges, originally roadside grazing from turnpike days.

At one time there is said to have been a toll gate at Furner's Green, south of Danehill, but no sign of this remains. The most notable building on this part of the road is the Sheffield Arms coaching inn. It was built two hundred years ago by the Earl of Sheffield to provide rest and refreshment for travellers on the Brighton road and has been said to have the "finest Georgian facade in England". There is also good original panelling preserved internally. With such fine features inside and out it may seem surprising that it has experienced a chequered history, with few people making a success of running it for more than a few years at a time. Local legend says that this is because of an old lady who lived in the neighbourhood and was thought to be a witch. On one occasion she visited the inn to ask for a drink of water – another version says she requested a lift on a cart, but whichever it was she was refused and, as a result, put a curse on the place that no owner should make a successful business out of the inn or stay there more than three years. The curse seems to have been successful as many different owners have run the inn over the years, none of them for very long. Its function as an inn has recently ceased, and it is now used as a business centre.

A toll gate stood at Sheffield Green. The gatekeeper here, as with all other gatekeepers on rural roads where the amount of traffic was limited, became very familiar with the particular riders and carriages that passed through his gate. In 1825 his observation was well rewarded:

> "In the dead of night between 29th and 30th March last, a man on horseback passed through the Toll-gate at Sheffield-Green, near Chaily, in Sussex; and the gate keeper recollecting that the same man had several times before passed the gate at the same unreasonable hour, every time on a different horse, conjectured that he might be one of those horse-stealers who had been doing so much business in that part of the country lately. He called up his father, living about 100 yards from the Toll-gate, and, after a short consultation they saddled their horses and galloped after the stranger. They overtook him about six miles off, at a place called Forest-row; and without much ceremony they told him what they thought of him. The stranger assured them that they were mistaken... the horse and everything about him was his own, he said, and he would give them proof of it if they would ride on with him to the next town. They agreed; but they had not rode far when, being better mounted than they were, he got ahead of them and presently saw him

dismount, abandon his horse, and scamper off on foot into the fields, where they soon lost sight of him. However, they caught the horse, which was the property of a Mr. Jeffry, of Chaily, and to have been stolen from his stable that night."

The horse thief was subsequently arrested and brought to trial at Bow Street. He had been stealing horses for sale in France.

On the west side of the road outside Sheffield Park, well hidden today amongst a tangle of undergrowth, is an impressive milestone nine feet three inches tall. It was probably erected about 1780, after the completion of Sheffield Park House, at the instigation of the 1st Earl of Sheffield. The south and north faces give distances to East Grinstead and Lewes respectively. Facing the road are, in addition, the distances to Westminster Bridge and Brighthelmstone.

Sheffield Park lies to the east of the road and has notable gardens, now under the care of the National Trust. The trees are particularly fine and are even remarked on in *Patterson's Roads*, where most descriptions are confined to the gentry rather than their surroundings:

"The soil in this part of the country is remarkably favourable to the growth of timber. Gough relates that, in 1771, two oak trees in Sheffield Park, whose tops were quite decayed, sold standing, at the risk of being unsound, for 69/-. They contained upwards of 23 loads, or 1140 feet of square timber. The carriage of them to the waterside, only nine miles, upon a good turnpike road, cost 30/-; each tree being drawn by 24 horses on a low carriage made for the purpose, and travelling only four miles and a half a day. They were floated from Landport, near Lewes, to Newhaven, where they were with difficulty embarked for the use of the navy at Chatham."

One of the delights of travel down the Brighton roads is still the sight of wonderful old oak trees beside the road. The story about the old oaks of Sheffield Park serves as a reminder of the many great oaks that were once a feature of the former forest. The mature trees we see today, perhaps 150 years old or even a little older, would have been dwarfed by the ancient giants. Nearly all, like those from Sheffield Park, were felled for their timber, and what an epic feat the transport of such mighty pieces of timber must have been. A great number of huge trees must have been available when Daniel Defoe made his tour in 1725. He refers to the timber being prodigious "as well in quantity as in bigness" and talks of seeing one tree on a carriage needing 22 oxen to draw it along. Such a tree could only be transported in short stages and it could take two years to reach Chatham. It was impossible to move such loads in the winter or even during a wet summer.

The road crosses the River Ouse at Sheffield Bridge. The river is some 20 feet wide here and lies a similar distance below the level of the modern road on its bridge and embankments. Even higher are the massive embankments further south, which carry the roads at the crossroads with the A272, a very wet and low-lying area. Work on raising road levels in this area commenced in the 1830s and has continued at intervals ever since. The road here crosses an area of common land and much of it still remains as open space. It can be considered a pleasant place for taking the dog for a walk on a summer's afternoon, or it can be seen with the eye of the traveller of two hundred years ago. At that time it was a low-lying region of rough grassland and marsh traversed by muddy streams; a summer pasture but a winter wasteland, a place to avoid or pass through as quickly as possible, albeit with some difficulty on the poor road.

After crossing another stream the road rises to the church and village green of Chailey. This area, and South Chailey, where there is also more common land, is not greatly changed from coaching days, but the course of the road has been altered from the original which lay along the eastern edge of South Common. The coach road through Chailey was well served with inns: the Five Bells is an attractive old building which was originally a local alehouse, extended after 1752 with the coming of the turnpike and the consequent increase in trade. The old road, now a track called Green Lane, is an attractive route which runs beside an old flint wall and over a hill which the new road avoids. At its southern end is another old inn, The Horns Lodge. Both these inns provided a change of horses. After Chailey the route soon runs downhill and onto the Weald Clay, a region of damp meadows where Bevern Bridge and Cooksbridge span two tributaries of the Ouse, after which the road approaches the South Downs.

The South Downs contains some of the loveliest spots in the south-east of England and it is always a delight to find the road rising up onto the chalk once more. Villages below the Downs have been comfortably settled there since Saxon times or before, watered by springs and rivers; sustained by the rich arable land of the scarp foot and by the downland grass and woodland on the slopes above. Offham is one such village, a pleasant place made all the better by the survival of an attractive toll cottage. It has been enlarged over the years but the original structure, brick-built with the usual projecting porch, is well preserved. A number of routes lead up the slope of the Downs from Offham, and probably more than one of them was used by coaches in the past. The present road is said to have been built originally by Napoleonic prisoners of war. It climbs up the side of the Ouse valley to reach the western end of the main road through Lewes.

So to Lewes itself, which provided another opportunity for refreshment as there was still more than an hour to go before reaching Brighton. The High Street is joined at its lower end by the road from Uckfield, and at its higher end by the road from Chailey. Lewes is a delightful place to visit. It is not made ugly with tasteless new buildings like Crawley and, in contrast to Croydon, the city fathers have felt their town's fine old buildings are worth preserving. Lewes was an important place in the history of the Brighton roads if only because it was the extension of the London to Lewes road that created the first recognised through route to Brighton. It has also always been important in its own right as a defensive site dominating the passage from the sea up the river Ouse, and as an administrative centre. Buildings and shops of all ages line the steep road up from the river, and the presence of a ruined castle confirms its historical authenticity. It lacks the big stores of the uniformitarian modern towns but its structure reflects the events of past ages. It is not boring. The Roman road, the London–Lewes way, was important throughout the Middle Ages. The coach routes from Wych Cross, which meet up here, were both important routes to and from London before Brighthelmstone had any more than local significance at all. The town commands an important crossing of the Ouse where firm land reaches the bank of the river. Above and below the crossing were and are extensive marshy lowlands. Many of the buildings would have been familiar to coach travellers, and many have flint walls and timber frames, while further walls of flint flank the old roads of the town.

On the southern side of the hill the White Hart is one of the most important of the Lewes coaching inns. Fine oak panelling has survived from the Tudor period, and in one of the panelled rooms the revolutionary Thomas Paine used to meet and debate with the Headstrong Club, which was formed at the White Hart.

Further up the High Street is a timber-framed fifteenth century building, now a bookshop. On its front a rectangular stone of late eighteenth century date gives distances from the Standard in Cornhill, Westminster Bridge and Brighthelmstone. Many other old inns, in addition to the White Hart, survive in Lewes, some with names changed since coaches stopped at their doors, but all originally serving traffic from London and, as it grew in importance, Brighton.

The Lewes–Brighton Turnpike Trust was established in 1770 and work on the new road started shortly afterwards. Before this, coaches took the old road over the Downs. As the first coaches of James Batchelar started operating in 1756 they must have used the old road for at least 14 years. This road turns left from Lewes High Street opposite the castle and then right along Southover High Street. This is another area of old houses, old flint walls and old inns. Just after the Swan inn the road continues as a track. Its course has been severed by the deep cutting through which the A27 now passes, but a bridge spans the gap and the track continues, gently climbing onto the Downs beyond Kingston. The steepest ascent here is up Castle Hill, from which there are wide views back over the lower Ouse valley. Lewes and its castle are seen with great clarity and the view would have been enjoyed by coach passengers who might, however, have been fearful of the "fearsome declivity" where the hill slopes steeply down from the track. This part of the road is still important as a bridle way and footpath, followed in part by the South Downs Way. It is still known as the Jugg's Road, a name which refers to the baskets, or jugs, of fish which used to be carried by fisherwomen from Brighthelmstone for sale in the market of Lewes.

The downland crest from Castle Hill to Newmarket Hill was all sheep walks in coaching days. Indeed, all the land between here and the coast supported such a great number of sheep that the area was known locally as "the mutton factory". Sheep still graze where the slopes were too steep for ploughing and the turf has been left unspoilt. It is good to see that the grass is being restored over some of those areas that have been unwisely ploughed over recent years. It is also heartening that here, unlike in so many places, the air can still be filled with the song of skylarks.

There are two dewponds at the top of the hill, and the old road runs past them. Many sections of the track are made of hard-packed flints, a good quality surface. William Stevenson, in his *Agriculture in Surrey* published in 1807, notes that heavy wagons quickly crush road material, including flints, to powder, but observes that "if a good coat of flints of a proper size be carefully laid on, mixed with a small proportion of chalk, the latter will cement and bind the flints after they are broken, and together they will form a very good road". The evidence for this is still there today on Market Hill and many other downland tracks. Over Market Hill are more wide views of rolling downland and, seen between the hills, glimpses of the sea. Soon Brighton appears and the old road descends to skirt the racecourse and continue into the town on the line of the present Elms Road. When the new turnpike was brought into use after 1770, the old road was abandoned by almost all traffic and the Downs remained the domain of sheep and shepherds.

This track is one of the longest surviving stretches of 'real' coach road – that is, a road which has been little altered; not built over and not given a modern tarmac surface. Such high and airy tracks remain today as a legacy of the past. Their abandonment in favour of the valley below means that they remain as places for walkers and horse riders to enjoy. Surely the good road and the wide views gave pleasure to our ancestors also. Probably, however, their main desire by this point on their journey was to stretch cramped limbs and have a good meal on arrival at Brighton. The new road which replaced the high, downland track follows a much lower-level route through the valley, past Falmar and with good views of the surrounding chalk hills. It has been much altered in recent years and the turnpike road has been obliterated beneath a soulless dual carriageway. Flowers sown in the verges are an attempt to improve its appearance but only in a small stretch of the turnpike, the section beside Housedene Farm, is the road in any way similar to the road which the coachmen knew.

There is, on this road, one important coaching relic which has survived from the 1770 turnpike. After coaches left Lewes they had to pass through the Ashcombe Toll Gate. This was an elaborate affair with a round building each side of the road. That on the north side was the main building, and was demolished shortly before the road was disturnpiked in 1871 and the line of the road moved slightly to the north. The southern building still stands away from the modern road, its bricked-up windows looking blankly east and west along the valley. It contains heating and cooking arrangements and may have been used for this purpose when the toll house was in operation. This was a particularly attractive spot in the past, with a stream flowing under the road from the north. The stream has now gone, except for a vestigial remnant south of the road, but the little round building is still there.

Toll gates provided an easily accessible and easily identifiable place for such occasions as hunt meetings, and Ashcombe was no exception. *Bell's Life in London*, for November 28th 1830, describes a fox hunt meeting at Ashcombe gate. Earlier, on May 9th 1824, a stag crossed the road at Ashcombe gate with the hounds in pursuit and ran into Kingston Combe. It finally "sought security on the summit of the Downs" but the report does not indicate its ultimate fate.

The modern road into Brighton passes Sussex University and continues into the town as the Lewes Road. The Bear inn stands beside this road where Erredge recounts, with sarcastic disapproval, that:

> "On Easter Monday, April 23rd 1810, the holiday folks, in all their Sunday finery, assembled in great numbers, as was their custom, at the Bear public house, Lewes road, on the ground contiguous to which they were entertained with the polished diversions of cock fighting and the baiting of a badger."

I think we can assume that this area was a less salubrious part of the town! The Bear was not a stop for stage coaches, although important locally. It did not possess extensive stables; only a barn at the back in which to put your horse.

So the countryside is left behind and the road passes into Brighton. The whole of this road from London is surprisingly varied and small parts of the old road have survived on each of the sand, chalk and clay. It has, of course, changed in many ways over time and there is plenty of evidence of where engineering has altered the gradient to make the roads easier. It is also obvious that the nature of road surfaces and the width of the roads has been undergoing constant change as well. Without these improvements no towns could have grown to what they are today, and Brighton was obviously no exception.

Throughout this description of the first of the Brighton roads we have used the term *road* in its modern sense, but originally the word did not relate to a physical structure at all but simply to a right of passage. Therefore something referred to in an old report as a road may, to modern eyes, appear to be nothing like a road as we know it. Modern roads, even those which we may call country lanes, are very different from their predecessors in many ways and one important aspect is their width. Before the gradual improvements in the eighteenth century the feature that we call a road was termed a highway, and there were three different kinds of highway – that is, roads which permitted general rights of way. The first type of highway was a *footway*, which was little, if at all, different from a footpath today. Next in importance came a *drift way*, a track suitable for passage on foot or on horseback and which, by an act of 1691, had to be no less than three feet wide. It was the equivalent of a modern bridle path. Important roads leading to market towns were *cartways*, with a minimum width of eight feet. All three types could be referred to by the misleading term of *highway* but often, particularly if sunken into the land, the roads were frequently impassable to wheeled traffic and even if a vehicle could get on to the road it could not easily pass another coming from the opposite direction. Roads between major towns were rather better, but Erredge, the Brighton historian, says of these early roads:

> "... the lanes and bye-ways being then very narrow, recesses in the hedge-rows were made in certain places to permit of the laden

> animals standing aside that they might be passed, as their packs, which extended considerably on each side of the animals, would otherwise frequently come in unpleasant contact with the fair sex, who on pillions occupied similar positions to merchandise when on horseback."

This description sounds similar to the narrow lanes with passing places that we are still familiar with in country districts today, but it must be remembered that Erredge was referring to most of the roads around Brighton in his time. At least in our age the fair sex is likely to be sitting comfortably in a car rather than slung onto a horse like merchandise! The roads around Reigate were particularly notorious for their narrowness. In 1755 Alexander Broughton told a House of Commons committee that the road south of the town was "in many parts so narrow that two carriages cannot pass nor a horseman pass a carriage".

The roads negotiated with such difficulty did not even take the traveller on a direct course towards his destination. Winding country lanes may have a certain rural charm but such narrow roads meant nothing but frustration to the impatient traveller between major towns. Dr Burton, in the same passage referred to earlier, says of Sussex roads:

> "No one would imagine them to be intended for the people and the public, but rather the byways of individuals, or, more truly, the tracks of cattle-drivers; for everywhere the usual footmarks of oxen appeared, and we too, who were on horseback, going along zig-zag, almost like oxen at plough, advanced as if we were turning back, while we followed out all the twists of the roads."

The problems with these roads were often due to the fact that maintenance was the responsibility of the parish through which the road happened to pass. The standard of surface required by local farmers driving their cattle was clearly different from what the long-distance traveller between towns needed. In addition, parishes seldom had the time or resources to do much in the way of road construction.

Anthony Bird, in *Roads and Vehicles*, records that a road maker employed locally in the eighteenth century was equipped only with a pick, a shovel, a wooden rake and a basket or a wheelbarrow. However industrious he may have been, his impact on a long length of road must have been limited. Some villages had a 'road plough' which was drawn by eight or more horses and was used every spring to draw the road material towards the centre. It was then harrowed to give a flat area for summer traffic. A steep camber was left on both sides of the road in order to shed water from the surface. This had the unfortunate effect of making an overturn by a coach more likely if it had to pull to one side. Where a surface on a minor road had been eroded down into the hillside over many years of use it was often left untreated so that loose debris would be washed down to where it could be conveniently shovelled away. Thus the road continued to sink even more rapidly.

The desire to improve such bad roads led to the setting up of turnpike trusts. Each trust was concerned with a comparatively local section of road, for example the Horley Turnpike Trust or the Reigate Trust. The roads managed by the trusts soon became known as turnpike roads, or simply pike roads. They were generally started by a group of local people, particularly landowners, who would benefit from getting their produce to market more easily. Others involved could be local justices, clergy and other professional people. To qualify, a trustee had to possess real estate worth £40 a year or personal property to the value of £800. The membership of the Reigate Trust, following the Act of 1755, is typical. It included several county gentry and local people of position such as Arthur Onslow, speaker of the House of Commons, Charles Cocks and Charles Yorke, the two members for the Borough, and the Rev. William Stead, the vicar. The powers of a trust lasted for only 21 years but they could be extended for a further period if the trustees wished.

When sufficient money had been subscribed and an Act of Parliament passed, work could go ahead. No doubt the trustees expected that when the road had been repaired, widened and straightened, and the collection of tolls had been organised, the road would pay for its own upkeep and provide a profit on their original investment. In the event, most potential profit was swallowed up in the cost of maintenance, but the founders of the trusts were more than compensated by the improvement of trade along the roads. An example of this can be seen in the road between Dorking and Horsham. Before 1755 the road had been a driftway, but it was improved to a cartway on being turnpiked. It is worth remembering that Dorking and Horsham were then, as now, important towns, yet before 1755, the road between them could be kept, legally, as narrow as three feet. It must, of course, have been wider than this or carriages and carts could not have used it, but only after 1755 was any improvement legally enforceable. Once it was improved the benefits were there for all to see. Arthur Young reported that the road was:

> "... no sooner completed than rents rose from 7s. to 11s. per acre; nor is there a gentleman in the country who does not acknowledge and date the prosperity of the country to this road."

The standards to which roads were constructed changed dramatically over the course of the eighteenth century. The first turnpiked road to be authorised in Surrey was under an act of 1696, to improve the road between Reigate and Crawley. This act gave considerable powers to improve the ruinous roads and to impose tolls. Most of the provisions were never implemented, but a new 'road' was made to cross the ten very damp miles between the two towns. This was the first road to be constructed in Surrey since the days of the Romans. It was intended only for horses, so would have been termed a driftway, wheeled traffic being kept away by the erection of posts at each end. Not until the turnpike act of 1755 was it widened to cartway status and thrown open to all traffic.

The width of later turnpikes was 18 feet for the actual road and further space was left for broad verges on either side, giving an overall width of 40 feet and sometimes even more. The verges often terminated in a ditch of up to four feet in depth and a bank surmounted by a quickset hedge. Some of the less altered sections of the roads to Brighton have retained their banks and ditches to the present time, now often hidden by trees and bushes but clearly visible when passing on foot, for example along parts of the road south of Danehill.

Road improvements by the early turnpike trusts consisted of little more than a certain amount of judicious widening and straightening and the filling in of ruts. This was commonly done by ploughing up the road and then raking it level. One of the first decisions of the Reigate trust was to hire teams for ploughing up the roadways at the rate of ten shillings a day for each team of a minimum of five horses. Presumably the surface was very soft after this treatment and would soon deteriorate again. Gradually, although rather later in south-east England than elsewhere, road engineers learned the techniques that enabled them to build roads with a more permanent surface. It even became possible to build better roads over the wet clay soils of the Low Weald. The methods applied with great success in other parts of Britain by Thomas Telford were not applicable to the Surrey and Sussex area as they relied on a base of large rocks which were simply not available. However, the other great road builder of the time, John Macadam, used smaller stones – "no larger than could fit into the mouth" – and he preferred to build on a soft base. The importance Macadam gave to the size of stones is clear. He is quoted by Copeland as saying, "I always make my surveyors carry a pair of scales and a six ounce weight in their pocket and when they come to a heap of stones they weigh one or two of the largest." The stones were laid as evenly as possible to a depth of six inches, and a further six inches was added a few weeks later. Such roads were cheaper to make than Telford's, and were the obvious method to adopt on the clay lands. Much interest was shown in Macadam's ideas and he visited Lewes in 1817 to attend a meeting with representatives of the turnpike trusts. This meeting led to a marked improvement in road building methods in the area.

The costs of road maintenance varied according to the amount of traffic and the type of surface. In *Agriculture of Surrey*, published by the Board of Agriculture in 1809, William Stevenson gives maintenance figures for different sections of road, averaged over the first seven years of the nineteenth century. Expenditure on the busy road between Brixton and Croydon averaged £154 a mile during this period. From Croydon to Godstone, where there was less traffic and the road was partly over chalk, the cost dropped by about two thirds, to £60 a mile. In general the underlying geology was the main reason why Surrey was the most expensive county for road building. There was no good stone apart from flint and even this was not readily available in many areas. Expenditure on less than three miles of damp land between Merton Bridge and the south of Clapham Common averaged in excess of £260 a mile over the seven years.

The trustees appointed to administer a turnpike act for a particular section of the road were granted wide powers. They could take land and materials from commoners without giving any compensation. Land and materials could also be requisitioned from private ownership, but this could only be done by order of a justice, and appropriate payment had to be made. Less was done to improve the passage across streams and rivers until the turnpike trusts had been established for some time. Although bridges existed on many roads the turnpike trusts were under no obligation to construct them. They only had to mark fording places with graduated posts driven into the stream bed near the deepest point of the ford.

Having made the roads, milestones had to be set up. This was not mandatory however, until the General Turnpike Act of 1766, which also defined the width of wheels allowed and fixed the weight of different classes of vehicles. Direction posts and fences had to be erected and quickset hedges planted. To the observer today, milestones are the most interesting of these requirements as they may still be found by the roadside. Many have unfortunately disappeared, notably in Sussex where they were removed at the outbreak of the Second World War and have never been replaced. A number have survived on the Brighton roads however, and their various styles relate to different stages of activity by the turnpike trusts.

Finally came the erection of toll houses, with their adjacent toll gates. These were generally simple single-storey constructions but some were more elaborate, following the tastes and fancies of their builders. The first toll houses were usually constructed of wood as it was thought they would only have to last the statutory 21 years, but as the terms of office of the trusts were extended more substantial brick-built toll houses were made. Just a few of these purpose-built toll houses have survived on the Brighton roads; for example the toll houses at Malling and at Offham. Others, which were originally roadside houses or inns and were adapted for toll house use, now remain as houses or inns once more. Not all the toll gates referred to in these pages were in operation at the same time. Some gates were closed and others opened as towns expanded and new roads were created.

Gates were erected across the road beside the toll house. The main gates were 12 feet wide; five- or six-barred gates. There was usually an additional smaller gate, three feet wide, for people passing on foot. One bylaw stated that they should be painted white and well lighted. The best lamps were "about 9 inches high and 6 inches wide in the clear; they cost about £1-7s each".

Many references are not to toll gates at all but to toll bars, and it is likely that most of the original barriers were bars, or 'pikes' which could be turned to one side, hence the term *turnpike*, which soon came to be applied not only to the gate but to the road itself.

Tolls varied considerably. On the early pre-Macadam roads higher charges were made for vehicles with narrow wheels. An Act passed in 1768 specified that vehicles with wheels less than six inches wide had to pay half as much again as the normal toll. Charges also varied according to the type of traffic; for example, at East Grinstead a horse was charged 1d., a one-horse carriage 2d., a coach 6d. and a wagon of hay 3d. Droves of oxen paid 2d. a score. The tolls were, of course, intended to provide money for the upkeep of the roads but the trusts made very little profit. This was not only because so much of the toll money was needed for road maintenance, but also because it was easy for the pike keepers to swindle the trustees who could have no knowledge of the actual amount of takings at each gate.

Not everyone paid tolls. Double tolls were often charged on Sundays, but churchgoers were exempt. Free from tolls also were clergy visiting the sick, the mails, those on military service and those going to vote in an election. Not surprisingly the payment of tolls was widely unpopular and was avoided wherever possible. Bars were erected on side roads to force traffic to pass the toll gate but little could be done to stop local people finding their own ways round by minor roads. Farmers would drive over their fields to avoid the gate and, eventually, landowners were subject to a fine if they allowed people to use their land to avoid the toll. However, most traffic preferred the wider and better-engineered turnpike roads and, by the 'Golden Age' of coaching, the toll gates provided a steady income for the trustees.

While road traffic continued to be very light by modern standards there was little need for regulation as far as driving was concerned. On roads to London there was an accepted custom, not always observed, that vehicles heading for the city took precedence over those going the other way. It was not until 1835 that an Act was passed making it a legal requirement to keep to the left.

Plate 17

The Sheffield Arms. A former coaching inn, said to have one of the finest Georgian facades in England.

Plate 18

Offham toll house. Still standing today, and lived in, unlike the majority of toll houses.

Plate 19

The Ashcombe Round House. This was one of two buildings; one each side of Ashcombe gate. The building on the north side was demolished to facilitate road widening.

Plate 20

Juggs Road. This road was the first coach road for London coaches via Lewes to Brighton. The road remains as this track which can be seen continuing up over the Downs after forking right.

Chapter 6
The Horsham Route: Kennington to Dorking

The road from London to Lewes was not the only well-established route that became, by extension, the Brighton road. The most westerly of the Brighton roads was another well-known way to the south and served such notable places as Epsom, Dorking and Horsham. For convenience it can be termed the Horsham route. Some of the traffic which crossed over Westminster Bridge and London Bridge was destined to turn aside at Kennington and follow this way south. In *Cary's Roads* of 1817 most Brighton coaches would have crossed the river at Westminster but at least two of the coaches heading for Horsham must have used London Bridge, both from Bishopsgate – one from the Vine and one from the Bull.

In his book *Thames: Sacred River*, Peter Ackroyd discusses the last days of the old London Bridge. The shops and houses that used to stand all across it were pulled down in 1760 to help ease the flow of traffic but the roadway of the old bridge remained in use until 1830. Traffic on the old bridge was counted on one day in July 1811. "It amounted to 89,640 pedestrians and 2,924 carts, 1,240 coaches and 485 gigs, 769 waggons and 764 horses." This enormous press of traffic was using the bridge despite the fact that it was not the sole crossing of the river. It sounds as if many of the vehicles were carrying goods rather than passengers but the number of coaches is still an impressive part of the total.

The Horsham route turned off from the road south through Croydon at Kennington Gate. This gate was described in Chapter One and was always a scene of hectic activity, particularly on Derby Day. There are more descriptions of this gate to be found than of any other gate south of the river. It was a place of frustration for drivers, entertainment for onlookers and memories for all.

On Derby Day a very large amount of the traffic was using the Horsham route as it crossed Epsom Downs. The *Illustrated London News* of May 31st 1845 refers to "Kennington of the remorseless pike and unstinted vocabulary" and rather ominously to its being the "Charybdis of Chariots". Even Lord Byron referred to the turnpikes glowing with dust. In June 1843 the *Pictorial Times* said of the Derby Day traffic:

> "The accidents were fortunately very few, but occasionally the coachmen would take it into their heads that a couple of four horse coaches could go through a turnpike-gate that was only large enough to admit one, and a crash would be the consequence.
>
> "At Kennington-Gate this circumstance happened more than once, the assembled crowds encouraged by their cheers those drivers who chanced to be more than usually dusty or desperate."

No specific accounts were recorded of travel to Brighton on the Lewes road but, for the Horsham route, there is *A Companion from London to Brighthelmstone in Sussex* by J. Edwards, published in 1801. Mr Edwards chose this way to reach Brighton and recorded many details of interest. After his comments on the Spread Eagle in Gracechurch Street already mentioned, he also tells us that the wells in the Brixton area had a mineral content and beers made with them would purge. Had he perhaps tried a local beer with unfortunate results? Another account of a trip to Brighton was written in 1789 by Henry Wigstead and illustrated by Thomas Rowlandson. The first part of their journey coincided with the Horsham route. Rowlandson's drawings are typically lively although subject to a degree of artistic licence. Wigstead is factual and boring. However, the two accounts between them make a very useful contribution to unravelling the story of the road.

The coaches heading west soon turned their backs on Brixton and its purging beers and proceeded down the Clapham Road. Some Georgian houses survive here from the days when coaches passed their doors but there is little else of interest apart from four milestones. They are cut square and must have originally been placed at half-mile intervals as they give distances to the half-mile to Whitehall and to the Royal Exchange. All four stand on the west side of the road, two on Clapham Road and one each end of Clapham Common. Two of the stones are of limestone; two of sandstone, presumably placed in position at different times.

The Clapham and Balham areas saw much housing development in the late eighteenth and early nineteenth centuries. Houses were first built on Balham Hill in the 1770s. Edwards has a number of references to "genteel houses" in Clapham. On Clapham Common South Side coaches stopped at The George, demolished in 1885. The Plough Tavern had, according to Edwards, "spacious and genteel assembly rooms, where all the gentry of the village and its environs hold their balls, assemblies etc. Here also is an elegant coffee room facing the road". Another inn, The Windmill, was "a very genteel and good accustomed house".

There is little of interest along Balham High Road and its continuation into Tooting. It is a well-used road, and was so in coaching days as well, but it was frequently avoided by coaches in bad weather. The nature of the surface was such that it became a mass of dust on a dry summer day and a deep layer of mud in the wet of winter. Coaches from the south would avoid it at such times by following Mitcham Lane to Streatham High Road. One report said of this route, "though round about, it was preferable to the unpleasantness of wading through the dirt and sand of Tooting and Balham". Other commentators were only a little more kind. In 1789 Wigstead and Rowlandson reported "... Upper Tooting; a delightful village – There is, however, beside its situation, nothing remarkable in it..."

At the northern end of Tooting High Street coaches to Sutton could turn off down Mitcham Road, but the road to Horsham and Brighton continued straight down Tooting High Street to Colliers Wood. This road was one of the many improvements after the 1755 Turnpike Act which upgraded it from its former driftway status – that is, with a minimum of three feet – to a cartway with a minimum width of eight feet.

The tolls set out in the Act emphasise the predominantly rural character of the area at that time. After the charges for carts and carriages the tolls for Merton listed:

"For every waggon, not laden with hay or straw: 3 pence and if so laden: 6 pence. For every drove of oxen or neat cattle after the rate of 2d. per score. For every drove of calves, hogs, sheep or lambs after the rate of 1d. a score."

The traveller is unlikely to see any droves of calves, hogs, sheep or lambs in Merton today, but will still see the River Wandle. Before the river crossing a drover would have had to pay toll at the first of the Merton toll gates. No doubt the Wandle was a very welcome watering place for the animals passing through. This gate was situated on the road from London just before it turns right to cross the river and become Merton High Street. At the other end of the High Street coaches turned left down Morden Road and passed through the Merton Double Gates, also known as Morden Gate. This crossroads is a busy place today and it was also busy in the past, as shown on a print from the *Pictorial Times* of 1845. Although the picture shows a fairly built-up area, its semi-rural nature is readily apparent, as is the dust rising from the road surface. Houses are certainly there but the scene is dominated by trees. This is countryside with urban encroachment still a long way from complete. One gate stood across the western end of the High Street before the crossroads, the other across the northern end of Morden Road. Coaches to Brighton would have expected little delay here however as a blue ticket issued at the first, or Single Gate, also gave passage through the Double Gates.

The Wandle at Merton is surprisingly wide: some 25 feet. For the coaches this was the first river to be crossed since leaving London. One reference to the Wandle in the local library serves as a reminder that rural surroundings could still mean danger from highwaymen as well as a road full of driven animals. In 1792 the *Times* reported that a highwayman had passed over Merton Bridge four or five times a week. The newspaper does not say whether he was eventually apprehended although it is noted that he was badly mounted. A poor horse surely means that he had found few rich pickings on this road. However, he had robbed one couple of 11 guineas at four in the afternoon while they were taking an airing in their carriage.

The crossing of the Wandle signals a change in the landscape; a change inevitably more apparent in the past than now but still clearly sensed by an observer on foot. This is the point where the coaches left the dusty roads of Tooting behind and entered a land of many streams and damp places. The present A24 follows the line of the old coach road and passes Merton Park. All travellers in the later years of the coaching age would have been well aware of the connections between Merton and Admiral Nelson, who loved his house there and referred to his "dear, dear Merton" when departing for sea before the battle of Trafalgar. Two streams flow west, the Beverley Brook and the Pyl Brook, eventually to join the River Mole. Three milestones survive here which vary so much in style they must have been replaced at different times. This replacement was presumably of milestones that had become defaced. That this action was considered necessary is a good indication of the importance of milestones in the days when coach drivers had no mileometer in the vehicle or other road signs to help them gauge distance.

The road down to Ewell and beyond was notorious for coaches racing each other in their eagerness to be first to Epsom and so the one most likely to secure passengers there. We can imagine them swaying down the road and splashing through the small streams, much to the consternation of their passengers. It was not so easy to race through the small town of Ewell itself however.

Parts of Ewell are still filled with the scent of water and this was even more extensive in the past, much of it the headwaters of the Hogsmill River. Coaches passed through a toll gate at the northern approach to Ewell and then the original road avoided the wettest land by turning left before the church, along Church Street and round a sharp left turn into the High Street. This turn became notorious. An account of Derby Day in *Illustrated London Life* refers to "Ewell of the fatal corner". Many accidents may well have occurred here as the Horsham and Dorking coaches raced each other but the worst accident occurred for a different reason, in 1826, when Walkers *Dorking Coach*, loaded with passengers, stopped in Church Street. The coachman had descended and it was his custom, when starting the coach after a halt, to stamp on the footboard as a signal to the horses. On this occasion a boy gave the signal while the coachman was still away from the coach and the horses started forward with no one in control. They turned too sharply into the High Street where the coach hit an iron fence and overturned. Some passengers were injured and others killed. One of the victims, 22-year-old Catherine Bailey, is buried in St. Mary's churchyard.

In 1834 a new road was opened between London Road and the High Street which avoided the fatal corner. This ground had not been used earlier because of the abundance of water there. At first horses and coaches had to splash through the ponds there, large parts of which still remain as an attractive roadside feature. It is easy to see what a barrier they were when at their full extent, before they were partly filled in to provide a safe route for the coaches. A milestone here shows 14 miles to London.

The rich, moist lowland around Ewell is delightful but, as on all the Brighton roads, there is something special in the landscape when the chalk lands are reached once more. Chalky soil soon appears south of Ewell as the road rises gently up to Epsom Downs. The Downs were, of course, the goal of the Derby Day traffic. The coach road is still followed by the present A24 and leaves the famous racecourse to one side. The roads that turn onto the Downs and racecourse are unremarkable today but were "disgraceful" in the past according to the *Sunday Times* on Derby Day, 1842:

> "Hundreds of carriages all rushing simultaneously, and making for the two narrow wretched roads which lead from the Downs to the road to London and to Epsom Town. These roads are a disgrace to the place; they seem laid down for the facilitating of accidents, – narrow, steep, crooked, and full of ruts and inequalities."

Epsom itself was always an important stop for coaches, even if they were not racing to get there, and there are numerous old prints showing coaches in the town. Many a coach could have been seen outside the Spread Eagle, which was the most famous of Epsom's coaching inns. It provided post chaises and saddle horses and was the stopping place for the Westminster coach from the Golden Cross at Charing Cross, and for a number of other London stage coaches. At first glance it seems that, like so many old inns, the Spread Eagle has been demolished, but it still survives as a building, with splendid carved eagles, wings outstretched, above each door. Unfortunately, although the building has survived, it no longer performs its original function, as it is now converted to a gentlemen's outfitters. It is sad that the inn as such has gone but well done Epsom for preserving this historic place with its eagles still looking out for the coaches that will never come again.

After Epsom the Dorking road soon reaches open country. In 1901 G. Home wrote of this road that it crosses the centre of:

> "... this breezy waste land, and then plunges precipitously downwards towards Ashtead. It is a pretty view from the top of the hill, with the white road running away from one's feet and disappearing at a bend among the trees below."

Various descriptions of the Brighton roads refer to "precipitous" descents in places where nothing seems particularly steep to modern eyes. Perhaps the term was used loosely, or perhaps the inadequate braking system on coaches was the reason for comparatively gentle slopes being thought of as steep. The view has changed over the last century. The "breezy wasteland" is much more wooded today and so the views are less extensive. The road still runs down the hill and disappears into the trees but the white chalk surface is now covered with tarmac. Home also remarks on the attractive pond and geese at Stamford Green. The pond is still there, and still attractive but, understandably beside the modern main road, the geese have gone.

Some coaches stopped at Ashtead to change horses at the Leg of Mutton and Cauliflower. Edwards noted that the coach from Horsham stopped there on its way up when a dinner was provided for the passengers. An old print of horses being changed at Ashtead shows what was a simple everyday scene in coaching days. The horses look tired and are being unhitched by ostlers and led away round the side of the inn for a well-earned rest. It is interesting to see from the print how many jobs depended on coach traffic at this one place. There are at least three ostlers at work and they are assisted by a man in a top hat; probably the guard. The coachman is also there, still seated on his box. On the coach there are four outside passengers, two gentlemen and two ladies. It is obviously a nice sunny day and the passengers are smartly dressed, all with hats and one lady with a parasol. What a clear indication of the gentle pace at which coaches moved! The passengers clearly had no apprehension that the wind created by their passage would in any way discommode them!

The next town on the coach route is Leatherhead. Today, the pedestrianised High Street has a pleasant feel about it and the absence of cars makes it easier to imagine the place when the only traffic was carts and coaches.

The original Leatherhead toll gate was in Great Queen Street (High Street). This gate was kept in 1772 by Sarah Firminger, who was paid ten shillings a week. She also received £10 a year for the printing of tickets. She was followed as gatekeeper by Thomas Wood, who seems to have had a hard time, or perhaps he was more conscientious than his predecessor. Henry Kitchen was fined £2 for assaulting the gatekeeper in the execution of his office, and later four other men were fined a total of £9.12.0 for assaulting Thomas Wood and passing the gate without paying toll.

The main coaching inn of Leatherhead was the Swan, the site of which is now occupied by a shopping centre. Many coaches stopped here and in 1791 it was said to be "a very genteel house with good accommodations, most excellent stabling and good post chaises with able horses to hire". A speciality of the house was fresh trout from the river Mole. The Leatherhead museum has a picture of the old inn and a battered stone swan which once stretched out its neck above the inn door.

Coaches had to turn sharp left outside the Swan into the Dorking road. This corner, like that at Ewell, was once the scene of a coach accident, but due in this case to poor control of his horses by the coachman. It was in 1806 when a coach carrying a party of ladies including Princess Caroline, the wife of the Prince Regent, to visit her friends the Lockes at Norbury Park, rounded the corner too fast and overturned. The ladies were thrown out of the carriage and, tragically, one of them was killed. The dangerous corner could probably have been avoided by then as an alternative road was built about the year 1800. This turned left before the old toll gate and curved round to join the Dorking road near the church as Church Lane. At the same time the toll gate was moved to a site just opposite what is now The Knoll, an area still marked by a space filled with trees and bushes, but there is no vestige of a toll house to be seen. The coaches probably still continued to use the High Street as they needed the services available at the Swan.

From Leatherhead to Dorking is surely one of the prettiest sections of any of the Brighton roads. The road goes down the Mole valley, first on one side of the river and then on the other. Walking along it is a pleasure, despite the accompanying traffic. The valley becomes narrower and the hills steeper on each side and then, as it enters Mickleham, the modern A24 swings away to one side and leaves the village in relative peace. Mickleham has been bypassed since 1935 and so it still retains much of its coach road atmosphere. Edwards described the Mickleham of 1801 as "a pleasant village consisting chiefly of one street, mostly good houses with pretty gardens behind them". To anyone walking through it, and also down the path to the fields behind, it is clear that this description is still exactly true today. In Mickleham, 'The Running Horses' was a posting inn but is also supposed to have been used by highwaymen. A very small ladder leading to the roof space may have been an escape route for highwaymen if required.

South of Mickleham is one of the best-known landmarks of Surrey. Box Hill rises steeply on the left. With the turnpiking of the road below it in 1775 it became a favourite playground for Londoners and has remained so ever since. The development of the road also saw the transformation of a local alehouse, the Fox and Hounds, into the Burford Bridge Hotel. Admiral Nelson and Lady Hamilton stayed here in 1801. There was only a footbridge over the Mole at that time so wheeled traffic had to use the ford.

With its relative accessibility to London, its peaceful countryside and its spectacular views, the Box Hill area developed strong literary connections. A guest at the Burford Bridge was John Keats who, while there in 1817, completed his writing of *Endymion*. The writer George Meredith lived at Flint Cottage at the bottom of Box Hill, and Jane Austen set a famous scene in *Emma* at a picnic on the hill.

The river Mole cuts into the slope of Box Hill and then swings across the valley to the opposite side, so the road has to cross it over Burford Bridge. The old road is now once more on the same line as the A24 and presents an unpleasant contrast to the Mickleham road. The original road followed the line of a river terrace which would have kept it safely above most flood levels. The modern road is raised even higher as the low-lying water meadows beside the river are regularly flooded in a wet winter.

There was a toll gate south of Burford Bridge at Gyles Green. This was situated just north of the turning to what is now Denbies vineyard, and just after the turning to Boxlands. Edwards refers to an inn called the Cock but the first edition of the Ordnance Survey 25 inch map calls it The Beehive. The building is now demolished but there is a photograph of it in the Dorking museum. The valley becomes wider at this point as the downland slopes fall back on either side. The coach road continued south to cross Pipp Brook, as does the present road. A new bridge was built here in 1786 to help the increasing amount of traffic entering the town. The road turned right beside the brook and then left to climb out of the valley, and finally turned right into Dorking High Street.

One of the most satisfying pleasures of exploring the old roads is to visit the fine old coaching inns where they have survived. Dorking holds one of the finest of all, the White Horse on the south side of the High Street. The White Horse became an inn in 1750 and was of great importance throughout the coaching era. It has the essential oak beams that everyone expects to see in such buildings and the whole atmosphere is redolent with the indefinable, but welcoming, smell derived from years of good service. There is a fine staircase which is a later addition to the building, but which is very much in keeping with the whole. At one time the White Horse was also famed for its garden where there grew a huge apple tree said to be the largest in the south of England. Edwards said the White Horse:

> "... is the least of the three inns in the town, but has the greatest share of business on market days, here are post chaise and saddle horses. The Brighthelmstone or Steyning coach always changes horses here and dines on going up."

It seems most unfair to use the term "the least" of such a fine inn, particularly if it had the greatest share of business. It certainly has no rival in the town today.

The coaches which stopped at such fine inns as the White Horse can easily become the subject of rose-tinted nostalgia and romance, and an essential component of that romance is the figure of the coachman himself. Unlike the nobility and gentry who rode behind them few coachmen have handed down their names to posterity, yet they must have been remarkable people, driving through all weathers and safely completing their journeys despite the deficiencies of the roads. Some names, however, have come down to us and various references give snippets of information about coachmen. A picture gradually emerges of what some of the occupants of the box seat were like. However good they may have been, the fact that they were remembered at all, not just in general but even as individuals, must be due to the intimate nature of coaching. The only comparison today might be with a taxi driver or perhaps a coach driver conducting a tour. In a similar way the stage coach driver was on the vehicle with you, sharing your journey, and his skill and personality directly affected your enjoyment of the experience. As with a modern taxi driver a coachman would expect a tip and usually this was well deserved. He might also supplement his income by taking on extra passengers whose fares he could pocket as their names were not on the waybill, an offence which was defrauding the coach company and possibly endangering the coach by overloading. A more serious offence was to accept a large tip from a wealthy young passenger to allow him to drive the coach for part of the journey. This was highly illegal as such young men would often try to drive too fast and sometimes overturn the coach.

The traditional coachman, who sat on his box whatever the weather, through the eighteenth and into the nineteenth century, was often the least attractive aspect of the whole equipage. He has been described as loutish and boozy, stout, red faced and hoarse-voiced. Much of this was probably due to the manifold discomforts of his job, and it cannot have been true of all coachmen, although the picture seems to be generally accurate. The 'stout' impression may have been reinforced by coachmen habitually wearing a 'double Benjamin', a clumsy and many-caped garment which at least had the virtue of giving substantial protection from the weather. Such protection was very necessary as most drove an average of 50 miles a day. Since changes of horses took place at inns, where drink was readily available, it is not surprising that many a coachman sought solace in the bottle. His appearance cannot have been enhanced by the custom of many coachmen of filing their front teeth so that they could use them to splice their whip points.

As the nineteenth century advanced, the image of the coachman changed and, from about 1820, smartness and gentility crept in. The smartness of the mails and their coachmen was certainly a factor in this; there are no records of any smart coachmen until the mails started. The chief reason for the change, however, must lie with the influence of the amateur whips, gentlemen who became interested in coaching. Coachmen who had been involved in teaching driving to a member of the 'quality' would subsequently ape their pupils in both manners and dress. The presence of such amateurs on the box seat of some regular coaches also provided an example in style which professional coachmen would follow.

By the time of the Golden Age, coachmen were frequently an adornment to their vehicles. They wore neat and colourful neckties, clean linen, top boots and a smart costume with huge buttons and a white beaver hat. With a posy in the buttonhole they were "as expert in folding a tie as in handling a team" and their box seat was covered with an attractively embroidered cloth.

As with car drivers today there was a fine mixture of abilities amongst coachmen. W. Outram Tristam, writing in 1893, has left a number of references to coachmen; he may well have actually been driven by some of them. He quotes Viator Junior on the poor driving of Brighton coachmen. Only seven of the 45 discussed were "artists" capable of "hitting 'em and holding 'em". He quotes another of Viator's accounts which, excluding unnecessary verbiage, describes a particularly bad coachman whom he must have been following along the road:

> "... he held the ribbons – also a cigar – between his teeth. He also had a pair of bad holders as wheelers... could not keep them to a canter. He was more successful in putting his chain down the hill by New Timbers, or this tale would never have been told except at a coroner's inquest... he let his team get well on to the crown of the hill, just before his change before he attempted to pull up when 'away they went'... by his awkward pulling and hauling, had the coach first of all in one ditch, and then in the other, till the passengers were utterly unable to say whether they were on their heads or their heels... At the very crisis of the affair the stables of the runaway team loomed into sight, when they stopped of their own

accord, in spite, no doubt, of the efforts of their driver."

This example of appalling driving clearly occurred above Newtimber, north of Brighton, on the Classic route. The original road here went steeply downhill, much more steeply than the modern road in its cutting, and it must have been an alarming experience to lose control there. One can imagine the passengers shouting at the coachman and angrily reporting his incompetence to the company, but there were no traffic policemen in those days and quite possibly no passing drivers to witness the incident apart from the man who recorded it. The coachman was probably able to continue driving his coach after being admonished by the owners.

Fortunately most records of Brighton road drivers praise their skill and in just a few cases we can see beyond the name and glimpse the man himself. Sam Goodman, who drove the *Times*, is mentioned as a good driver by a number of writers, as is 'Young Cook' who first drove the *Magnet* and afterwards the *Regulator*. He was "not only a first rate coachman but one of the pleasantest fellows to travel with that could be met with on the road". Another fine driver according to Viator was "the incomparable Mr. Snow, whose perfect ease and elegant attitude on his box in turning the *Dart* out of the Spread Eagle Yard in Gracechurch Street was a sight for gods and for coachmen". This reference is probably to Bob Snow, one of two brothers, Robert and William. They became partners with the great coach proprietor William Chaplin, working from the Spread Eagle in London and the Blue Coach Office in Brighton. Chaplin and Snow had five coach yards in London: at the Spread Eagle, the White Horse in Fetter Lane, the Cross Keys in Gracechurch Street, the Swan with Two Necks in Lad Lane and the Angel behind St. Clements. In 1834 they had between 1,300 and 1,500 horses and 64 coaches. With income from the coaches and the inns they made over £500,000 a year, a truly enormous sum at that time. Such wealthy coach owners were a minority however. A local innkeeper might own just one share in one coach.

Amongst an earlier generation, Thomas Crossweller was a fine driver on the Brighton road at the close of the eighteenth century. He also became a coach proprietor and shared the business at 44 East Street, Brighton, which later became the Blue Coach Office. Crossweller drove with William Hine, another particularly well-respected driver, known as 'Old Hine' to distinguish him from later drivers of the same family. Hine is said to have driven over 100,000 persons to Brighton without ever an accident. He is said by Bishop to have been "universally liked and whether as regarded skill, good humour, strict integrity, or a desire to promote to the utmost the comfort of his passengers, few could compare with him". The traditional coachman in appearance, if not in manner, Hine wore a huge 'box-coat' of seven capes which he would lend to notable passengers on his coach.

Henry Hine, William's son, was another distinguished driver. He drove two-horse coaches for Mr Hyde in the early nineteenth century. At the last turnpike before Brighton old Mrs Loveday, who lived there, would always bring out a nosegay for Mr Hyde. Henry Hine wore high boots and a neckerchief that was as large as a fair-sized tablecloth and had to be folded on the kitchen table. He always drove four bays while his cousin drove four greys. Unlike the generality of coachmen, Hine eschewed deep drinking and hard swearing.

While discussing the coachmen we must not forget the presence of guards. These were employed on coaches from the mid-eighteenth century onwards, but not on every coach. No doubt they included many worthy men but they lacked the glamour of the coachmen and their names have not come down to us. Guards must have become very tired while executing their duties as they often stayed with the coach for its entire journey, many uncomfortable days on a long route, while the coachmen seldom did more than 50 miles at a stretch. There was, of course, no need for a change of coachmen on the London to Brighton route and the guards on this route were more fortunate than their long-haul brethren. The duties of stage coach guards were similar to those on mail coaches. They were responsible for the protection of the passengers and their luggage, for oversight of the waybill (the list of passengers booked for the journey) and for assisting the coachman with skidding and unskidding when going downhill. On the approach to a toll gate or to a change of horses, the guard had to sound his long horn, the traditional 'yard of tin', so that the coach's needs would be promptly attended to. This changed after 1818 however, when the key bugle was introduced from Germany. The new bugle became very popular with the guards and, as there were no regulations restricting its use by stage coach guards, some of them became quite proficient at playing tunes.

The least recognised, but surely the most numerous, group of drivers on the roads was the wagoners or carriers. Little skill was needed to drive the slow, lumbering wagon and they could not aspire to the elegance and efficiency of stage coach and mail drivers, yet they must have been tough, capable men. We think of carts and wagons as mainly utility vehicles employed on the farm or transporting goods around the local area, but must remember that they were important for a great deal of longer distance transport also. P. G. Lucas, in the *Danehill Historical* magazine of 1991, gives an example of this. William Wood, the landlord of the Sheffield Arms, ran a carrying business also. In 1855 a relative, Vince Wood, left Brighton at 8am on Tuesday and spent the night at Fletching. On Wednesday he drove to the Sheffield Arms, East Grinstead and London. On Thursday he returned from the Half Moon Inn in the Borough back to the Sheffield Arms. On the Saturday and Sunday he was again driving between Brighton and East Grinstead. This was all with a heavily loaded wagon on inferior roads, and exposed to whatever the weather might have in store. Life must have been one of unremitting toil.

Mr Wood seems to have been a very capable driver but not all wagoners were as good. There are records of wagoners descending hills without proper control, being grossly overloaded and, a frequent misdemeanour, riding on one of the shafts. Sometimes they were in trouble for "furious driving". This does not mean that they were going too fast – for most wagons this would have been an impossibility – it simply means driving with little control. Of course, as with newspapers of any age, it was the bad drivers who got reported. The vast majority of good, competent men were not news. Despite its mundane nature, however, a passing wagon could be made attractive both to see and hear. The paintings of John Constable explore their picturesque quality and in the museum at Cuckfield there is a delightful feature of wagons on display. The museum has two sets of wagon bells. Each set consists of four bells which all ring different notes. They were fastened to the horses or to the wagons themselves and would chime as the wagon and horses swayed on their way. They must have made a pretty sound while also warning other vehicles of their approach.

Stage coaches were also dressed up to look more attractive at certain times of the year. In the spring, particularly for May Day, the coachman would decorate his whipstock with coloured ribbons and bunches of flowers and would wear a huge nosegay on his coat. The guard would wreath his horn with blossoms and more flowers and leaves would be draped over the coach, almost obscuring the view through the windows for the inside passengers. The horses too had new harnesses and saddlecloths, wreaths of laurel on their heads and brightly coloured rosettes.

Coachmen, like any other specialist trade, developed their own vocabulary relating to their work. A short list is given by John Copeland in his *Roads and their Traffic*. An empty coach was "a mad woman", asking passengers for money was "kicking them". A passenger who gave no tip was said to be "tipping the double" and a bad coachman was a "spoon". Horses were "cattle", a horse given to kicking was a "miller" and if you galloped your horses you were "springing them".

There are few coaches or coachmen in sight outside the White Horse today, yet surely their ghosts must still pass down Dorking High Street, seeking for further signs of the town they had known. Another inn which still stands is the Bull's Head in South Street, which is shown in a painting by a local artist displayed in the Dorking museum. As with so many paintings of towns in the coaching age two obvious differences from today are the general lack of traffic and the loose nature of the road surface. A coach stands beside the inn and a new team is being led out for a change of horses. A few people, a cart and some dogs make up the rest of the activity in the street. The whole impression is of a gentle rural calm. Walker's coach was operated from here and catered for people wanting an evening in town. It left Dorking at 3pm and arrived at the Golden Cross, Charing Cross, at 6pm. There were stops at the Spread Eagle, Epsom and the Angel, Tooting. Return was the following morning at 9am to reach Dorking by noon. The cost of the journey was half a guinea. This was the coach that stopped operating after the tragedy at Ewell.

One of Dorking's inns has now been converted into shops, notably a bookshop at No. 39 High Street. This was once the Wheatsheafe, and its former status as an inn is clearly apparent. The archway under which coaches would pass still leads to a courtyard where stands a mounting block to assist horse riders. The greatest interest is below ground, however. Here there are passages and cellars carved out of the soft sandstone rock beneath the inn and extending under the High Street. One small circular cellar, now partly blocked by masonry shoring up the building above, is the site of a cock pit. The heat, noise and excitement must have been tremendous in such a confined space and, no doubt, the patrons were in frequent need of refreshment supplied from the rooms above.

A further claim to fame of the Wheatsheafe was the rearing of gigantic hogs, surely a more intriguing sight for the curious than the great apple tree at the White Horse. In 1750 it housed the largest hog in England, which was 1,036 lbs. in weight. This monstrous beast was sent to be exhibited in the West of England from whence it never returned, the hog and its minder having apparently vanished – no easy feat, one would have thought! Giant hog breeding cannot have been stopped by this setback, however. An even larger one was housed at the inn c. 1767 but sadly it broke a leg and had to be killed. Even though this occurred before fattening to maturity the animal was found to weigh 1,456 lbs, was 12 feet long and had a girth of eight feet. It was subsequently stuffed and kept on display at the inn. What a pity it is there no more!

The coach route through Dorking turned left out of the High Street into South Street, where it passed the Bull's Head and so on to the Horsham Road. The toll gate here was known as the Harrow Gate. The original gate stood opposite the junction with Hampstead Road but was removed in 1857 to beside the Bush inn. The gatekeeper's cottage here was on the opposite side of the road.

MORDEN GATE
(Panorama of the road)
1845

Plate 21

Morden Gate, otherwise known as Merton Double Gates. One gate crossed the western end of Merton High Street and the other the southern end of Merton Road. The scene is somewhat less rural today!

Plate 22

The White Horse, Dorking. One of the finest of the surviving coaching inns.

Plate 23

The Bull's Head. Dorking was an important stop for coaches before the long journey over the clay lands further south.

Chapter 7
The Horsham Route: Dorking to Brighton

The road south from Dorking went down Flint Hill, where there is now a roundabout at the point where the old road is crossed by the A24. The coach road continued through North Holmwood, where the large green and pond are still much as coach travellers would have seen them, but the local people no longer graze their geese and cattle on the grass in front of their cottages. The road originally climbed past the church and its route is now followed by a footpath. It climbs steeply through the trees and joins the modern A24 at Mid Holmwood where it becomes entirely subsumed by the dual carriageway, a fast route for motorists but an abomination to the senses of the pedestrian walking beside it. Fortunately traffic can be escaped at many points by walking into the woods alongside. There are delightful walks here, with good vistas through the trees and woodland valleys cut by small streams. As the noise of traffic fades it is replaced by the call of birdsong, yet is it really the landscape coach travellers would have known? The area is known as Holmwood Common and, according to Edwards, used to be famous for holm oak trees and for fine red deer. However, he says that by 1801 the trees had been cleared and replaced by furze. All grazing ceased in the 1950s and as a result the trees are now returning, but will red deer ever again be grazing in this part of Surrey? It seems unlikely with the A24 traffic thundering through and an urbanised countryside not far away. Whether trees or furze, Holmwood has always been an area of wild country and it used to be an area where highway robbery was frequent. Probably furze was preferable to the forest as there would have been less cover for robbers to use near the road.

Modern roads are good at obliterating evidence of their coaching history but just past Mid Holmwood, there is a memorial stone set back from the western side of the road. On it a metal plate is inscribed:

> "In memory of Alfred Gwynne Vanderbilt, A Gallant Gentleman, A Fine Sportsman, who perished in the Lusitania May 7th 1915. Stone erected on his favourite road by his British Coaching friends and admirers."

Vanderbilt was a great coaching enthusiast who wanted to bring back the glamour and nostalgia of the coaching age at a time when coach services had already disappeared from most roads including, of course, all the main routes between London and Brighton. He decided to use the Horsham route, pointing out that, "this road, being a longer route, is avoided by direct London to Brighton traction engines and motor traffic". He first advertised the service in 1910 as leaving London at 10.15am and stopping for lunch at the Burford Bridge Hotel for 70 minutes, finally arriving at Brighton at 5.30pm. Vanderbilt ran his coach, the *Venture*, until the start of the First World War when his horses were requisitioned for the use of the army. He was drowned when the Lusitania was torpedoed, having given his life jacket to a fellow passenger, a woman with her baby.

The Holmwood Gate, at Holmwood Corner, lay just by the small stream which marks the boundary between Dorking and Capel parishes. A plan of this part of the road, which is held by Surrey Record Office, shows what an isolated spot it was, with no other buildings nearby. It provided a lonely living for the gatekeeper, one of whom is recorded as being either very brave or very foolhardy, and he deserves to have his courage recorded. One night he was confronted by a gang of smugglers bearing kegs of brandy and, upright citizen that he was, he refused them passage through the gate. The reaction of the smugglers is not known but the gatekeeper was certainly fortunate to live to tell the tale.

Dramatic incidents like this were rare, stories to be told at the alehouse with increasing embellishments as the years passed. Minor misdemeanours were far more common at all toll gates. In 1775 six farmers were fined for avoiding payment of tolls at the Holmwood gate and in 1779 two carters were charged 16 shillings "for riding on their wagons on the turnpike road contrary to the Act of Parliament".

Just south of Holmwood Corner the line of the coach road can again be followed on the minor road which passes Holmwood Station. This road passes a splendid large pond before again being obliterated by the present A24. A short distance further south and, once again, the coach road is bypassed by the A24 and can be followed down a pleasant road through Beare Green and Capel. Another large pond just after Beare Green is attractive with water lilies, and one of many in a landscape which is a countryside of ponds. These were, of course, important as a source of water for livestock and were vital for drovers with herds of cattle. Surely they must have also provided welcome variety to the view for coach travellers on their weary journey.

Reference was made in Chapter 5 to the improvements which started on the Dorking to Horsham road after the Turnpike Act of 1755. It is almost impossible to visualise how this road, a fast dual carriageway as it is today, was little more than a cart track before that time. Despite there being many settlements along it, the status of the road until the 1755 Turnpike Act was only a driftway, meaning that the minimum width could be as little as three feet. Even the section of coach road which leaves the A24 and winds down to the village of Capel is a much wider road than it was when the first stage coaches used it. At least this is a quiet country road and provides a pleasant way into the attractive little settlement of Capel. There are many old timbered buildings, including the Crown public house, a place full of historic character with wonderful old oak beams. Beside the village street a limestone milestone has survived which shows it is 29 miles from Westminster Bridge.

Where the road runs south to Capel it passes over a small rise, which is of some geographical significance. To the north, all the streams flow into the River Mole but, from now on, rivers as well as roads head towards the Sussex coast and their waters at this point drain into the River Arun. As the rivers change, so does the county. We move from Surrey into Sussex and pass places with the name 'Shiremark', including Shiremark Farm. There is now no indication of whether there was once a physical mark to indicate the boundary.

The toll gate at Kingsfold was the first Sussex gate to be reached on the Horsham road, and stood just north of the road junction. Today there is a house called Milestone Cottage, but no milestone to be seen. A metal milestone south of Kingsfold gives distances to

London, Dorking, Horsham and Brighton. Completely different in type from that in Capel it is the only readable milestone on this road in Sussex. There is another of the Capel type, but minus its metal plate, in Horsham.

After Kingsfold the road, awash with traffic, continues through moist, low-lying countryside. It is much more pleasant when the A24 turns away from the coach road, just before the A264 junction. The old coach route goes along Daux Hill and the clump of woodland to the west of this road is still known as Coachroad Clump. The coaches then turned east towards Warnham Mill and passed Warnham Mill Gate, shown on the 25 inch map of 1875 as a small building surrounded by fields. Warnham Mill Bridge, and the old flour mill itself with its enormous mill pond, is still a very pretty area today.

Coaches could avoid the centre of Horsham and head straight for the crossing of the River Arun at Tan Bridge but most would have headed for the centre of the town. Here, beside the Carfax, is another of the famous coaching inns of the Brighton road, The King's Head. At such an inn the peace of the countryside was exchanged for noise and bustle and the comforts of the inn contrasted with the discomforts of a dusty, swaying coach. No wonder so many writers recorded their favourable memories of coaching inns, even though their meals may have had to be rushed at times. In 1801 the London coach left the King's Head every Monday, Wednesday and Friday, at 6am in the summer and 7am in the winter, to arrive at the White Hart in Southwark about eight hours later. It returned on the following day. The King's Head is certainly one of the best of the Brighton road's surviving coaching inns. Like the White Horse in Dorking it has lots of old timbers and the unmistakeable atmosphere of a coaching inn. Part dates from the Middle Ages and part is Tudor. As well as the beams and oak panelling there is a minstrels' gallery. It is easy, when sitting in these surroundings, to visualise the coach passengers staying there and to imagine coaches pulling up at the door. In the later days of coaching the passengers may have been slightly disconcerted by the words *Inland Revenue Office* prominently displayed on the front wall. The taxmen had an office at the inn and when they left, in 1881, their sign remained on the wall and it is still there today. Appropriately the inn is roofed with Horsham flags. This is a sandy limestone that was quarried locally. The heavy slabs are frequently seen on old buildings in the vicinity and require timbers of massive strength to support them although, even so, some old roofs may be seen sagging beneath the weight.

Two different roads continued to the sea from Horsham and either could be used on a journey to Brighton. The first of these to become established was through the important small town of Steyning. Much of the way is over low-lying clay but, after crossing the Adur, the Downland chalk provided a firmer surface. The first regular Brighton coach on this route was started in 1780 by Tubb and Davis from the Spread Eagle in Gracechurch Street. This was helped by the fact that the road between Horsham and Steyning, via West Grinstead, had been turnpiked in 1764, when the standard was improved to that of a cartway. It is significant that Tubb and Davis are the same coach proprietors who ran a Brighton coach through East Grinstead and Lewes. At that time this was the only other practicable coach road through to Brighton apart from the Lewes route.

The toll gate to be passed by coaches leaving Horsham for Brighton by way of Steyning was on Picts Hill, half a mile to the south of Tan Bridge over the River Arun. The river has carved out a deep valley here which meant that, as usual, coaches had to deal with very steep slopes down to the bridge and up again. The modern bridge is at a higher level with the river a long way below. The gate was part-way up the slope to the south of the bridge and, because of the slope, was the scene of a number of accidents. One of the worst accidents concerned a travelling salesman named Langley who was driving an open carriage pulled by a "mettlesome" young horse. He offered a lift to Mrs Sayers, a farmer's wife, who accepted it against her husband's advice. On reaching Picts Hill, Langley tried to halt the horse in order to fix the skid pan on the rear wheel, but the horse reared and then bolted. They crashed into the gate, smashed the cart and the horse was killed. Langley and Mrs Sayers were thrown out. Langley died immediately and Mrs Sayers shortly afterwards.

A lift in someone's carriage was, of course, normally every bit as straightforward as a lift in a car today. Thoughts of danger and accidents were far from the minds of the people involved. However, the unpredictable nature of horses was always a potential hazard. The combination of a "mettlesome" horse, an inexperienced hand at the reins and the steep gradient of Picts Hill were a likely recipe for disaster as, presumably Mr Sayers well knew!

The gate on Picts Hill was known as Horsham Gate. A ticket bought there also opened the next gate on the road, Bines Bridge, near the old Partridge Green railway station. At one time the gatekeeper at Horsham Gate was Mrs Jane Hill, who also supervised Bines Bridge, about eight miles away, which was kept by her blind husband. He sometimes had his grandchildren to help him but, even when on his own, he managed to keep accounts with local farmers by using a square stick for each one, cutting notches in the angles to record when they had passed the gate. Some of these sticks are said to have been in the Horsham museum, but they seem to have been mislaid over time. In 1796 a barracks was built beside the road between Tan Bridge and the Horsham Gate. It provided accommodation for soldiers in the Napoleonic War and was demolished in 1815. While it was in operation the town of Horsham suffered greatly from the activities of the soldiers, with riotous behaviour, robbery, assaults and street fights. During this period an extra toll gate, Tan Bridge gate, was established to take the toll of those visiting the barracks but not continuing through the Horsham Gate.

The road south after Picts Hill went through Southwater, where a sandstone milestone survives but is now totally illegible. The coach road then rejoins the noisy modern A24 for a few miles before turning off left to West Grinstead, from which point it becomes a delightful road across undulating countryside. It crosses small streams flowing to the west branch of the River Adur and the line of the South Downs now marks the horizon. Partridge Green Gate was south of the village of that name and stood on its own amongst the fields. This gate is also known as Bines Gate because beyond it is Bines Bridge, which carries the road over the Adur at the limit of tidal water. The river is 30 feet wide here and the flood plain protected by substantial levees. The risk of flooded roads must have been considerable in coaching days and this could well have been the type of country where a pair of oxen were needed to drag the Shoreham to London coach.

Bines Green, south of the river, has an overgrown pond and old cottages scattered along the open space. It is one of those points along the road which seem little changed and give a glimpse of the roadside of the coaching age. A cow and a few geese on the open grass beside the road would make the picture perfect. The road continues over very low-lying damp country with particularly wet ground in many of the fields and woods near the road between Partridge Green and Steyning. It is an attractive undulating road with fine views of the South Down ahead, but it would have required expensive maintenance, for example where the road is on a terrace well above the very marshy Wappingthorn Wood. It is easy to see why, in the days before better surfaces could be built, oxen were sometimes needed to pull vehicles out of the mire. The wood lies north of the minor crossroads which was the site of Wappingthorn toll gate. Soon after this another stream was crossed and the coaches entered Steyning.

Steyning is one of the most attractive towns on the various Brighton roads. It is full of lovely old buildings with walls of local flint and heavy old timbers. The High Street is a delight and Church Street possibly even better. One fine old inn, The Chequer, is a friendly place with the expected oak beams and a particularly fine wrought iron bracket for its inn sign. Post chaises and saddle horses used to be available at the Chequer, and cock fights were staged at Easter and Whitsun. The rival establishment was the White Horse. The present White Horse replaces a building burnt down in 1949, partly utilising the stables of the old inn. Edwards remarks:

> "The air of this town and country is allowed
> to be very wholesome and its inhabitants in
> general long lived."

Past Steyning is more damp land, with a pond beside the road. Bramber is soon reached, another place of remarkably attractive old timbered houses. There was a toll gate at Bramber, the toll house of which is said to have been partly incorporated into a hotel. It has little resemblance to the old toll house, of which a picture survives. Bramber gate was reported in Pierce Egan's *Life in London*, April 1st 1827, as the place of death of a stag, one of those unfortunate beasts that were caught and then released at a pre-arranged spot for the gratification of huntsmen. On this occasion the animal clearly refused to cooperate:

> "A considerable muster of high and low life
> took place at the Devil's Dyke yesterday,
> under the supposition that the celebrated
> Derby Stag, Robin Hood, would again be

turned out there; the time mentioned was mid-day, at which period a cart, with a stag in it, did appear, not, however, the redoubted Robin but the sluggish beast that had disappointed a very numerous field on the Ditchling Hills only a few days before. Long faces now became general, and half crowns were more difficult in collection than on the preceding occasion. The animal was let down, but some time elapsed, when he carefully shaped a leisurely course into the Devil's Dyke Valley followed by divers sportsmen and the Harriers... He crossed about 40 yards of Mr. Walter Burrell's estate, at a canter, and then trotted to Beden, and on to Bramber Toll-gate, in all about 5 miles; when about half the pack came up with and secured for the spit, it is hoped, as the only way in which it is likely that he can produce wholesome or agreeable diversion in the future."

A very different event at the Beeding Gate is reported in the *Sunday Times* of May 23rd 1841. Once again the courage of a toll gate keeper was tested:

"Attacks on Toll-gate keepers, for the purpose of robbing them, are becoming very general in Sussex... On Monday night another attack was made at Beeding-gate. It appears that the keeper, who was an elderly man, was knocked up by three men who, on opening his gate, laid hold of him and aimed a blow at his head, which he fortunately avoided, and only having his shirt on he broke away from them and succeeded in closing the door, which they attempted to break in. The gate-keeper warned them that he was prepared with a double-barrelled gun (which he loaded), and would fire at them if they did not sheer off, after some time they left."

The Beeding Gate was situated nearly opposite the present Rising Sun public house at the southern end of the Henfield road. The old building was destroyed when a lorry crashed into it but the remains were rescued and the toll house can now be seen re-erected at the Weald and Downland Museum at Singleton.

The Adur was crossed, as now, at Bramber Bridge and then, at this the earliest opportunity, the road took to the chalk hills. What a relief it must have been for coachmen to move onto the hard chalk after the heavy pulling through miles of road on clay. The road here, up Beeding Hill, is one of the best examples of an unchanged coach road to be found on the Downs. It is more rutted than it would have been in coaching days, but in places a surface of compacted flints has survived. Although the hedgerows have been allowed to encroach too far across the verge it has really changed very little over the last two centuries. The few farm vehicles that use it still disturb clouds of dust if they pass on a dry summer's day. The road would have been a steep pull for horses; probably passengers would have had to get out and walk, but surely the walk would not have been too unpleasant when it was accompanied by wild roses and the scent of thyme.

The view from the top of the hill is well worth stopping for and has changed comparatively little. New roads and new buildings can be observed in the distance and some former downland now bears arable crops, but there are also the grassy slopes of sheep-dotted hills and the description by Edwards in 1801 is totally accurate:

> "Top of Beeding Hill, from which is the most amazing view of the lower country. You look down the steep of this hill into the wild, quite another region beneath you; and a vast range of many miles of enclosure are walled in by the sweeps of bare hills projecting in the boldest manner, a view uncommonly striking."

The coach road turned right at the top of the hill and kept to the crest of the downs as far as New Erringham Farm. Here the more direct road to Brighton swung left to pass east of Slonk Hill and down to Kingston. This road, including the way up Beeding Hill, was turnpiked in 1807 but disturnpiked again when the new road along the Adur valley was constructed. Parts of the road can still be seen as sections of the bridle way from Erringham Farm to Kingston. Erringham Farm itself served as a coaching inn at one time. Most coaches, however, preferred to carry on over the downs to the south to Old Shoreham in order to pick up and set down further passengers. There were other routes to Brighton from the top of the hill but these were not used as regular coach routes. One, of which only some sections remain as footpaths, eventually joined the main turnpike near Brighton at Goldstone Bottom.

On both these roads the song of skylarks fills the air, as it did in coaching days. Wheatears would also have been a familiar sight; still today they flit from fence post to fence post ahead of the traveller. This bird used to be trapped in the summer months by downland shepherds who made a valuable addition to their income by selling them in large numbers to wealthy gourmets, for whom they were a particular delicacy. The bird nests in holes, such as rabbit burrows, and it also seeks such holes for shelter. The shepherds would make shelter burrows for them in which they would place a snare.

After the wide open downs, coach and horses would descend to Old Shoreham along Mill Hill and pass along The Street. Here there is a wonderful wall, 18 feet high and built of whole flints. The wall is the highest free-standing flint wall in Sussex and is a listed Grade Two structure. Coaches turned round by the Red Lion inn, a very old building where the low ceilings and ancient beams can still be enjoyed. From here the coach road followed the line of present roads through Kingston, Southwick and along the present A270 to the junction with the Dyke Road and so into Brighton. This road was newly constructed in the 1780s after the old coast road was washed away.

A robbery which occurred on the night of 30th October 1792 links the Red Lion and Goldstone Bottom. The mailbags from Horsham through Steyning were carried that night by John Stephenson, a boy of 12. He rode behind the Brighton coach which, at that date, would have been following the road past Erringham to Old Shoreham. The postmistress, who was a passenger on the coach, sent Stephenson another way across the Downs to Brighton, by the route which took him straight down to Goldstone Bottom before joining the turnpike road. It happened that two criminals, Edward Howell and James Rook, were waiting there to waylay a farmer who was expected to return that way from Brighton with a large sum of money. In the event, the farmer changed his plans and stayed the night in Brighton but John Stephenson rode straight up to them and was robbed of the postbags even though they contained only half a guinea and a letter. Stephenson managed to reach a nearby farm and raise the alarm. Rook went to the Red Lion where Phoebe Hessell, a famous old character locally, heard Rook boasting that he and Howell had stolen half a sovereign from a man carrying the mails at Goldstone Bottom. She gave information to the authorities and Rook, a simple and normally inoffensive character, was arrested. He confessed and implicated Howell. They were executed on 26th April 1793, being hanged publicly at the site of the robbery where their bodies were left suspended in iron frames from a 25-foot gibbet until they decayed. A macabre and sad ending to the story is that Rook was only 24 years old and his mother would come from her home in Old Shoreham to collect her son's bones as they gradually fell to the ground. She put them in a chest and buried them in Shoreham churchyard, determined that, even if illegally, her son should lie in hallowed ground.

Much of the track that Stephenson would have followed has now been obliterated under road and housing developments, but part of it remains as a terrace way amongst the trees of Three Corner Copse. The Goldstone, a large piece of sandy conglomerate, stands amongst ornamental flower beds where the track meets the road from Old Shoreham. The stone used to stand on the west side of the valley about three hundred yards from its present position, and has been repositioned. When it was simply an isolated stone in a wild valley it would have provided an appropriate atmosphere for dark deeds.

There is no doubt that, despite its scenic attractions, the climb over Beeding Hill was the most serious obstacle to coach traffic on this route to Brighton. For centuries it had been impossible to build a good road on the flat land of the Adur valley as it was too wet and liable to flooding. Eventually, however, advancing techniques of road building made it possible to construct a new road to Old Shoreham on the land below the hills and beside the Adur. This is the line followed by the present main road. It was different from all previous turnpikes to Brighton as it was a completely new road throughout its length, turnpiked in 1817. Up to this time all others had been based on the improvement of existing roads and tracks. Nearly all traffic made use of the new road immediately and the

Beeding Hill track became almost deserted. Just south of the junction of the Steyning and Henfield roads near Upper Beeding is a house called Toll Cottage. This is where the toll gate was located on the new road.

There is nothing particularly dramatic about the wide, flat valley of the River Adur. If the modern traveller's eyes stray from the road it is probably to look with pleasure at the soft lines of the hills that rise to east and west. It is, however, particularly significant that the earlier coaches avoided the valley floor. Coaches could struggle through clay and up hills but in conditions of flood they were helpless. The River Ouse is bridged at Lewes, the Adur at Bramber. From either of these bridges the danger of floods is obvious. Upstream the floodplains stretch for miles, while downstream are damp fields and, since the rivers are tidal here, extensive salt marshes.

Even when crossing smaller rivers it was not unknown for coaches to become stuck in the muddy waters. If this happened the unfortunate passengers had to get down from the coach, possibly into water and mud approaching waist deep, and wade to safety before the vehicle was light enough for the horses to pull it to drier ground.

On most river lowlands, whether the roads were good or bad, the hazard of floods figures prominently in travellers' tales and in coaching prints. A "seasoned traveller" is quoted by N. C. Selway as saying:

> "Give me a collision, a broken axle and an overturn, a run-away team, a drunken coachman, snowstorms, howling tempests; but Heaven preserve us from floods."

There is no mention of any specific flood to which the writer was referring, but it had clearly made a deep impression.

The alternative route from Horsham to Brighton leaves the town centre along the line of the present A281 and passes through about 20 miles of lovely countryside, and much of it avoids the worst horrors of busy modern roads. In spring the hawthorns are heavy with blossom and the roads are fringed with hedge parsley. On days like this a seat on the roof of a coach must surely have been a happy place to be despite its inherent discomfort.

This route became popular after the road from Handcross to Henfield was turnpiked in 1770. The Horsham to Lower Beeding road was turnpiked to link with it in 1782. Henfield, on its own, did not have the passenger potential provided by Steyning and Bramber but it now became a significant stage on one of the Brighton roads.

The route here is crossed by many streams, headwaters of the River Arun, which have been dammed to create hammer ponds for the Wealden iron industry. This road must have been a difficult piece of engineering. All the stretch past Manning's Heath and Lower Beeding as far as the Crab Tree public house is on heavy weald clay. This in itself, as we have seen, was a very difficult road foundation but the situation was made much worse when streams such as these were so deeply incised into it.

Heavy clay is ideal land for oak woodland and there are fine old oak trees growing beside the road. Some of the oaks which once grew here have provided timber for the structure of the Crab Tree. At this inn a copy is preserved of auction particulars from when the inn was sold in 1896. By this date the railway age was in full swing and even the first cars may have made their tentative way past, but many items in the auction relate to the horse-drawn trade. There are three carts, a gig and a truck, plus equipment relating to them: iron carriage stands, axel stands, iron carriage jacks, tyre benders and a smith's bellows. Fifty years after the end of the stage and the mail we can still see the extent to which the trade of the country inn was dominated by horse-drawn traffic. The inn dates back at least to the sixteenth century, and the Crab Tree toll gate stood just north of a minor road to the east. It is remembered by the name of Toll Gate Cottages at the roadside.

The road continues almost due south, through Cowfold and to the site of the Corner House toll gate which was situated just south of the junction with the road to Partridge Green. The building that served as a toll cottage is still there. The eastern arm of the Adur is crossed at its tidal limit less than a mile south of here, and then at the junction with the Albourne road was the Crouch Hill gate. The toll cottage and its garden lay in the angle of land made by the Cowfold and Albourne roads and it is said that, until at least the 1970s, the garden enclosure could still be seen but there is no trace of it today. Across another, smaller river, the road enters the locally important town of Henfield.

Henfield is a pleasant small town and holds much of coaching interest. Until recently a patch of coal dust stained the pavement outside one building. This was the entrance to a working blacksmiths', typical of what was once one of the most frequent and important establishments on all coach roads. Here in Henfield it survived as a working concern, standing on the same site it had occupied for centuries. Sadly the working forge has now gone, and has been transformed into a private dwelling. There is no call for fixing iron tyres onto cartwheels nowadays, but a metal disc is still set into the pavement on the opposite side of the road. This was used for shaping the tyres to the exact form to fit a cartwheel.

There are a number of buildings in Henfield from before and during the coaching age and, as always along a coach road, the most important of these are inns. One inn of much interest today is the George. It has developed around a thirteenth century hall, has fine old beams and an open fireplace. Some post horns on display are not from Brighton coaches but the inn was a coach stop as well as providing post chaises and saddle horses. Upstairs it is possible to see where beams in the wall have extensive burn marks on them. This was the result of rush lights being placed too near the wood in days gone by. Judging by the marks, the George must have come close to being set alight on more than one occasion. The George had a reputation for good, prompt service. One reason why this was possible was because stable boys were set to keep watch across Henfield Common from the yard at the back of the inn so that, when a coach was seen approaching in the distance, all could be made ready for its arrival.

The Prince Regent was one traveller who changed horses at the George. The story is told that he arrived at the inn one day and liked the look of Jimmy, a young post boy who was putting in the fresh horses. Holding up three half-crowns he told Jimmy he could have all three if he could get to the Black Horse in Horsham within the hour. Jimmy managed the ride with ten minutes to spare and afterwards was always asked for by the prince.

The other important coaching inn at Henfield was the White Hart. Henfield is the place where the Vanderbilt coach, referred to earlier, was forced to finish its days. On the very day that war broke out in 1914 the coach had got as far as the White Hart when it was stopped and had its horses commandeered for military purposes. Is it not of some comfort to know that ours is not the only age when unreasonable and high-handed actions can be taken by minor officialdom? I am sure the passengers would have felt the country could have survived without those particular horses until they had been allowed to reach their destination.

The coaching inns served many vehicles but one above all, the mail coach, embodies the glamorous image of the coaching era. Yet, from its inception in the last decades of the eighteenth century to its extinction by competition from the railways, the mail coach ran for no more than 60 years.

In the early days mail was sent by adapted stage coaches, but soon specially designed coaches were used. Innovations in the design of mail coaches led the way in coach building. The first specifically designed mail coaches were used from 1787. They were awkwardly high, but were the first to have the boot attached to the body. The coaches were designed and built by John Besant, who joined with Vidler and Co. of Millbank. After Besant's death Vidler continued to make and improve the coaches. The attaching of the fore and rear boot to the coach meant they were now much more comfortable for the coachman and guard as they could benefit from the springing of the main coach body. Other improvements were also made. The coaches were rented by the post office from Vidler at a rate of two pence halfpenny per double mile – that is, the journey out and back. This paid not only for the use of the coach but also for servicing it. According to Anthony Bird in *Roads and Vehicles* these "servicing agreements were vigorously enforced and so admirably executed that the mail coach standards of efficiency and smartness could be matched only by the richest and most fastidious private owners of carriages".

By the early 1800s the improvements in coach design had produced lower and safer mail coaches and outside passengers were now accepted, one next to the driver and one behind. None were allowed at the back with the guard until the late 1830s as it was feared that the guard might be overpowered by passengers who were criminally inclined.

Regular servicing meant that the mail coach was not only safer than the stage, but always presented a smart appearance. All, including those on the Brighton road, had red wheels and the lower coach panels were a deep maroon. The boots and quarters were black, with the four orders of chivalry being painted on the quarters. Below the windows were the words *Royal Mail* and the names of the towns at each end of the journey. This contrasted with the shabby appearance of many stage coaches which were often a garish yellow or blue with the name of the proprietor and the destination painted on them. Even the horses with the mail coaches were smarter and better cared for than those pulling many a stage.

The mail was carried in a locked box upon which the guard rested his feet at the rear of the coach. Nothing else could be carried there; all passengers' luggage had to be fitted into the fore boot. Inside passengers were limited to four and, with only a few outsides, the mail coach was much more lightly loaded than the stage, which could often be carrying as many as 15 passengers. The lighter load was certainly one reason why the mail coaches could travel more rapidly.

Speed was important for the delivery of the mail and it was helped not only by good design and fewer passengers, but also by the length of the distance between changes and the time taken over the change. Mail stages were seldom more than ten miles long and the average was only about eight and a half miles. The frequent changes meant that the coach was pulled by fresh horses for more of the journey than was the stage coach, but more changes meant that they had to be done very rapidly or the advantage of fresh horses would be lost. Five minutes was reckoned to be enough time to change a team of four horses and those in charge at the inns had to be reported if the horses were not ready immediately the coach arrived. The written instructions issued to every mail coachman stated "it is the Coachman's duty to be as expeditious as possible".

Once the roads had been improved, mail coaches could run at up to an average of 13 miles an hour on a good stage. Only the very best stage coaches could match this. The mail was helped by certain legal advantages over the stage coach, however. Turnpike gates had to be opened, at any time of day or night, when the guard of the approaching coach sounded his horn. The coach could therefore pass through at top speed without slowing at all. This was possible because the mail coach was exempt from paying toll. Also, on the open road, every other vehicle had to move to one side and make way for the mail. Drivers who did not obey this rule could be prosecuted, but they would be let off if they signed a public apology to be displayed in post offices nationwide. The shame of such public abasement proved to be an excellent deterrent to bad drivers and was much cheaper than taking them to court.

Mail coaches ran at night, and almost all of them, and certainly those to Brighton, left London at eight in the evening. Night running was only possible when road surfaces had been improved and this was done partly at the insistence of the mails. Of necessity the mail coaches were brilliantly lit and must have been a startling sight as they passed through the dark countryside of that pre-electric age. All coaches had at least two lamps, and in the case of many coaches five, which were said to cast a dazzling illumination on the highway. According to Harper, writing long after the great days of coaching but when those days still survived in living memory:

> "These radiant swiftnesses, hurtling along the roads at a pace considerably over ten miles an hour, were highly dangerous to other users of the roads, who were half blinded by the glare, and, alarmed by the heart-shaking thunder of their approach and fearful of being run down, generally drove into the ditches as the least of two evils."

For many years the mails were the fastest coaches between major towns, but they gradually lost this supremacy as stage coaches improved in design and the methods of operating them became more efficient. Despite their speed between stages, they were inevitably delayed at intervals by post office business and so could not always have a fast change. Travel at night also became much less popular with the public when day coaches started to rival the night mails in speed.

The coachmen and guards themselves were strictly supervised to make sure that the high standards of the post office were maintained. In his excellent book on the mail coach service Edmund Vale quotes a letter, sent in the year 1800, to mail contractors from Thomas Hasker, in charge of the mail service:

> "Sir,
> Stopping at Alehouses on the Road between Stage and Stage, under Pretence of watering Horses, but in Reality to drink, have been found very detrimental to the service; I have, in Conjunction with many Principal Mail

Coach Contractors, determined to annihilate so shameful a Practice, and I have my Lords the Postmaster-Generals' Commands to send the enclosed Letter to all the Guards, and this to you, desiring you will immediately give full Directions to your coachman not to go into, or even stop at such Houses – it is only done (under Pretence of Necessity) to carry on bad Commerce, to the injury of yourselves, by illegal Practices of taking up Passengers and Parcels which are never accounted for.
I am.
Sir,
Your most humble Servant,
T. Hasker."

There is no doubt that such "shameful practices" must have been commonplace amongst the majority of coachmen and guards. It is hard to blame them, as a glass of ale must have been truly necessary after a hot and dusty stage. Most stage coach proprietors probably turned a blind eye but the post office were determined to check such goings-on. Certainly the postal service was well disciplined in every particular, and, as a result, its coaches reigned supreme.

A final, but important, point to be made about the mail coaches is their excellent timekeeping. With the advantages they were given on the road they had everything in their favour, but the main responsibility for their regularity lay with the guard. The guard's seat in the boot was known as the 'dickey', and here he sat with the two outside passengers on the roof facing him. He had a number of very specific duties and one of these was to ensure good timekeeping. Towns on the route kept what was known as Local Apparent Time, which was taken from a publicly available clock, usually on the church, and maintained as to accuracy by a local clockmaker. There was, of course, some variation in this time along the line of the route so the guard was issued with an official clock which he had to carry. It was in a locked, glass-fronted box which the guard had to sign for at the start of the journey. Subsequently the time at every post house had to be signed for once the post master had checked the clock. The post office could therefore check whether the coach had run behind or ahead of its scheduled time and ensure that it had not arrived too early for a change of horses in order to contrive a few more minutes' drinking time. If time was being lost, and the guard felt it necessary, he could order out extra post horses and charge the cost to the contractors. These measures resulted in the mail coaches becoming so punctual that, in many places, the local people relied on the arrival of the mail to check the time rather than the church clock.

The guard had a number of other important duties. He had charge of the waybill, which gave details of passengers and their luggage, and he was responsible for the passengers themselves if protection was needed against highway robbery. To protect the mail and passengers he had a blunderbuss, a pair of pistols and a cutlass. When the coach was going downhill the guard had to jump down and operate the shoe to prevent the coach running away if the horses could not hold it. He had to sound the horn when approaching a toll gate or an inn where a change of horses was required. Mail guards were not allowed to play tunes on the newly introduced key bugle. Those who wished to do so would, however, sometimes purchase them secretly and play them when well outside London.

There was no lack of applicants for the post of guard, and they were carefully selected. The guard had to be literate and had to prove that he was under 30 years of age. If successful he had to spend two weeks with Vidler's at Millbank to learn about coach construction, as one of his duties was to undertake roadside repairs if these were necessary. On the occasion of a breakdown, the coachman's duty was to the horses. One attraction of the guard's job was that he was issued with a free new uniform every year. It consisted of a hat and a scarlet tunic frogged with gold lace, and was much prized.

For much of his journey the guard must have been extremely bored, sitting on his own at the rear of the coach and shivering in the cold night air. He was busy at stops or when operating the shoe on hills, but he had no continuous occupation like the coachman who had to be attentive to his horses all the time. Sometimes, however, excitement took the place of boredom. On July 16th 1827 a notice from the General Post Office stated:

> "Whereas on the Night of Thursday the 12th instant, about a Quarter past Ten o'clock, the Driver with the Mail was felenously stopped by

> two Men on the King's Highway, between Leatherhead and Dorking, opposite Givon's Grove, when the Men fired two Pistols at the Driver, and seriously wounded him.
>
> "A Ramrod was found near the spot, and is supposed to have been dropped from the Pistol of one of the Offenders."

It seems most unfair that the Post Office make no mention of the guard, who would certainly have been present. However, one of the attackers dropped his ramrod and there is no mention that the mails were stolen, so it seems probable that the guard was successful in driving them off.

The worst tribulation for the guard on the mail coach, as well as for his stage coach colleague, may well have been the length of his journey. This contrasted strongly with the situation of the coachman. The coaches were horsed by mail contractors, usually stage coach proprietors, and the coachmen were employed by them. The coachman was responsible for the coach and the passengers, but only for his stages which never totalled more than five hours.

The guard was employed by the post office. His prime responsibility was for the mails and it was his duty to ride on with them if, for example, the coach was held up by snowdrifts. He could be on duty for 12 hours continuously, a length of time which could easily encompass the whole journey. The guard was, however, particularly welcome at stops because, due to his longer journey, he could bring news from more distant places than could the coachman and he was always awaited at stops along the way as an important purveyor of news. It is reported that during the trial of Queen Caroline "all along the line of the mails, crowds stood waiting in the burning sunshine for the news of the trial, which was shouted out to them as the coach passed". Also, during the different stages of the Reform Bill of 1832 people waited beside the mail coach roads to hear the latest news shouted by the coachmen and guards.

Brighton coaches of all varieties turned left after Henfield and crossed the expanse of Henfield Common, much of which remains unchanged today. It must have been a splendid sight to watch a coach and four approaching over this open and gently undulating road. It was probably coaches here that were remembered by Mr N. P. Blacker, surgeon of the Royal County Hospital, from his boyhood in Fulking. He vividly recollected seeing the coaches at night:

> "... when the approach was announced by the bugle, and they were lighted up with a number of lamps, and seeming to bear down upon you like a big ball of fire..."

The common is a pleasant place to walk on a sunny summer's day but, even in country districts like Henfield, there could be danger in the air when crossing such places by coach at night. A toll gate barred the road at Terry's Cross near Woodmancote, and here a violent robbery took place in 1849. In January of that year the head clerk of Griffiths' Brewery in Brighton received a letter saying "Some parties intend to rob you next time you goes to Horsham, so bee on your guard." On 6th February Griffiths decided to go to Horsham himself. He hired a gig and, on his way back from Horsham, stopped at an inn in Henfield where he showed the landlady two pistols, only one of which was loaded. He set off in bright moonlight and passed Terry's Cross gate at 9.05pm, but he never reached Dale Gate, the next gate on his route. A shot was heard at about 9.30pm, which must have been the one that killed him, and his body was discovered the next day with the loaded pistol still in his pocket.

A little over a mile from Terry's Cross the road bends sharply to the right. A road goes straight on here to link up with the A23, but this was not built until 1808 when it immediately became the main road. Earlier coaches followed the road along the lower part of Newtimber Hill and then faced the hard climb to Saddlescombe. A toll gate stood at the bottom of the hill, just to the north of the turning-off to Poynings.

The long pull up to Saddlescombe would have been very tiring for the horses, and also for the passengers who would probably, as usual, have had to get out and walk. The reward at the top was wide views across the Downs and the first sight of the sea as an indication of journey's end. Much of this land is under plough today, but would have been entirely sheepwalks in the past. The good surface of a chalk track would have been welcome but the place is bleak in winter, very exposed to whatever the weather may offer.

The descent down the Dyke road into Brighton was an easy end to the journey but a long haul for coaches on their return. It is joined by the road from Old Shoreham, and they descend as one into the town. On the left is the parish church of St. Nicholas. Here is the tomb of Phoebe Hessell, the same who recognised the robber, Rook, at Old Shoreham. When still a girl, aged 15, she had disguised herself as a man and enlisted in the Fifth Regiment of Foot to follow her lover, Samuel Golding, to the West Indies. She fought in various campaigns and was injured by a bayonet at the Battle of Fontenoy in 1745. Later she was posted to Gibraltar where her sweetheart was injured and sent home to England as an invalid. Phoebe then told her commanding officer of her sex and was also discharged home. She married her lover on her return to England and, on her husband's death in 1792, she married again. She lived to be 108 and attended the coronation of George IV.

Plate 24

The old coach road over Holmwood Common. There were fewer trees and more scrub and open areas in coaching days, but the common provided ample cover for highwaymen and was also a haunt for smugglers.

Plate 25

The smithy at Henfield was one of the last to survive on the roads to Brighton. Until recently, this was still a blacksmiths', but sadly it is a smithy no longer, and only its sign remains on the wall.

Plate 26

The *Venture* coach outside the White Hart, Henfield. This was the coach run by Alfred Vanderbilt just after the First World War, and Henfield the place where its venture ended, when the horses were requisitioned for military service.

Plate 27

The Chequer Inn yard in Steyning. The Chequer still survives and this view from the yard towards the street has changed very little.

Plate 28

Bramber toll gate. The narrow road with only one cart in sight was typical of country turnpikes, and even of small towns.

Plate 29

Beeding toll house, now re-erected at the Weald and Downland Museum, Singleton.

Chapter 8
The 'Classic' Route: London to Crawley

When Charles Harper wrote about the Brighton road at the end of the nineteenth century he was exploring the 'Classic' route, the road through Sutton, Reigate and Cuckfield; the road already referred to as "The Appian Way for the High Nobility of England". This was the road of Regency romance. It was the road for high society between London and the sea. The road upon which could be seen the flower of English nobility with their servants and their carriages, their peers and their hangers-on. It was the road where the noble and the fashionable of England followed their prince to the balls and assemblies, concerts and cockfights, the sea air and the sea bathing. It was the place to see and be seen, in the new and exciting town by the sea which was soon to give its name to the road leading south from many other towns: the Brighton road.

Other routes were older but had really only become Brighton roads by accident. Brighton was merely an extension after their goals of Lewes or Horsham or Steyning had been achieved. The Classic route had been fairly important as far as Reigate but, as a way to the sea, it owed its existence to the development of Brighton. The road as far as Reigate had been turnpiked in 1755, and parts nearer London even earlier, but much of the way further south was hardly developed at all. Problems with wet clay soils were very great and, until the development of Brighton, there was nothing to make the most direct route to the sea an economically desirable enterprise.

The first part of this road was the same as the Horsham route as far as Tooting, at which place the Classic route turned left along Tooting Broadway and round Amen Corner, then went south to Mitcham and Sutton. According to Edwards in *A Companion from London to Brighthelmstone in Sussex*, the Mitre at Amen Corner was a meeting place of the Beefsteak Club, alternating with the

Wheatsheaf at Tooting. It was called Amen Corner because the house was formerly kept by the clerk of the parish. Milestones, originally one every half-mile, continue the series found in Clapham. They were first set up in 1745 but a good number of them must have been altered or replaced at later dates, as there is variation in them between limestone and sandstone and also between Roman and Arabic numerals.

There is little of coaching interest in this rather featureless area but today an open area of land remains at Figges Marsh, a name with various spellings including Pig's Marsh, and beside this damp area another toll gate was situated. The gate was near a milestone, now completely obliterated, which lies at the northern end of the former marsh; another of the 1745 series which, like the others, formerly gave distances to the Royal Exchange and Whitehall. The road continues directly south from here to Mitcham. In the *Illustrated London News* of May 31st 1845 there is an engraving of 'Figs Marsh Gate' on Derby Day. A horse is rearing up in the shafts while a stout gentleman tries to control it. Another horse looks as if it is about to expire, while a group of locals look on placidly. The trees in the background suggest an extensive area of open country.

When Harper was writing, one hundred years ago, Mitcham was famous for the cultivation and distillation of lavender and many other scented plants. *Patterson's Roads* states that "a vast quantity of medicinal plants are cultivated here". The scent that wafted in the air would have been familiar in coaching times as this was an entirely rural area, well away from the built-up regions of London. Mitcham was a very important place on the coach road. There were 11 inns to serve coaches, the most notable of which were the White Hart and the King's Head, now the Burn Bullock, overlooking Lower Green. A particularly well-preserved milestone still stands across the road from The Cricket Green whereon cricket matches have been played for over two hundred years; another sight well known to passing coaches.

The River Wandle, famed in the past for the excellence of its trout as well as the many mills built along it, is crossed south of Mitcham and the road passes over Rose Hill, past a milestone of 1743, to Sutton. Here, as around Mitcham, rural tranquility prevailed and the old coach road was skirted by fine elm trees.

Henry Wigstead described Sutton in 1789:

> "This village is very pleasantly situated; and the Air is so pure and healthy, that with the additional inducement of eating the celebrated Banstead-Down Mutton, many citizens of London resort here on Sundays."

The 1743 milestone stands opposite the end of Benhill Avenue but, apart from that, there is little to see of the "pleasantly situated village". Today shops line each side of the hill and there is a modern shopping mall thrown in for good measure. Sutton is prosperous and busy, a pleasant enough shopping centre but holding very little of the coaching age. There is, however, at the top of the hill a sign depicting a cock. There it stands on top of an iron pole beside the site of a famous coaching inn of that name which was eventually demolished in 1898. Edwards said that the Cock inn "may be justly deemed one of the first inns on this road between London and Brighthelmstone". There is an often-reproduced print which shows a substantial building with a gallows sign across the road. A coach stands in the yard and another is approaching. Four people admire the action from the upstairs windows. The Cock was certainly one of the most familiar stopping places for coaches, remembered with affection by many coach passengers as one of the places where Banstead Downs mutton could be enjoyed, if the coach stopped for long enough to allow passengers time for a meal. It was also famous in its day for being kept, after his retirement from the ring, by 'Gentleman' Jackson, pugilist and champion of England. His very presence was, in itself, sufficient inducement for many sporting gentlemen to stop at the Cock to refresh themselves. The other principle coaching inn at Sutton was the Greyhound which, like the Cock, had a sign right across the road.

In 1772 toll gates and a toll house were erected outside the Cock. Sutton Hill Gate controlled the main road and the side roads to Carshalton and Cheam. These replaced an earlier gate a little down the hill to the north. The cost of building the toll house sounds impossible to modern ears: a mere £82.

In Edward's time, 1801, common fields lay to the south of the Cock but, as Sutton grew in size, in 1836 the main gate was moved further south to Sutton Lane, near the twelfth milestone. This stone, nearly opposite Egmont Road, was erected in 1746 and still stands, having seen the toll house come and then pass away. Many improvements were made to the roads in Sutton as the years passed, and Sutton became a larger, more significant place. A major improvement was to the formerly low-lying area around the end of the present Cedar Road, which was known as 'Foul Slough' and had been, for generations, an ordeal in wet weather. The mud here was made worse by traffic from a nearby chalk pit. There was another very wet area by the Cock inn. Improvement work took place from 1813 and further work was undertaken to drain water from part of the High Street. Local people, who had had to put up with roads of mud all their lives, must have been pleased that the increase in coach traffic had, at long last, stimulated some action to rectify the problem.

When toll gates were generally abolished, and the Sutton Lane toll house was closed, the contents were sold at an auction held on 13th February 1882. The auction catalogue of materials and fittings is kept at the Surrey Record Office. The following items pertaining to the road are extracted from the list and are no doubt typical of the majority of toll gate appurtenances along the Brighton road:

"1. Iron Bedstead.
2. Road hoe, 2 pick axes, iron rake and fag hook.
3. Road hoe, rake, trowel and pail.
4. Road hoe, rammer, short ladder and harrow wheel.
5. Wire sieve, 2 lanterns, ½ yard measure and 2 brooms and various others 14 lots...
19. Strong navvy barrow with iron wheel...
23. Patent road scraping machine...
25. Strong iron bound snow plough...
37. A 11 ft painted oak gate, with long iron bolt, catch and hinges, and hanging post 5 ft long.
38. A 10 ft 10 inch ditto and ditto.
39. A 10 ft 3 inch ditto with spring catch and hinges.
40. A 3 ft 9 inch swing oak gate with hinges.
41. A 3 ft 3 inch ditto with post...
43. A 11 ft iron lamp post.

44. A 10 ft oak post for lamp and bracket ditto framed white board, size 3 ft 6 inches and 2 ft 6 inches wide.

It appears from this that the gatekeeper had more to do than just collect the tolls. He was also expected to maintain the road and to clear snow when necessary.

A picture of this gate and toll house, held by Sutton library, shows a wide gate spanning the road beside a two-storey house. The print was made in 1865 and a few houses in the background show that Sutton had spread this far south by then.

Inevitably, newsworthy events recorded along the road are often the result of criminal activity. As with other areas, Sutton had its fair share. One incident became very well known, perhaps because it was more audacious and better planned than the usual hold-up by a highwayman who simply made off with the purses of the travellers. The occasion was the theft of between £3,000 and £4,000 from the *Blue Coach* on February 5th 1812. The Brighton Union Bank had a box beneath the seat of the *Blue* which they used when transferring cash to and from London. On the day in question the money was placed in the box as usual before the coach left London, but on arrival in Brighton that evening the box was found to have been broken open and the money removed. The coachman stated that six passengers had booked inside places on the coach. Two, a gentleman and a lady, were there from the start of the journey, two more gentlemen were taken up on the road and the other two never appeared. At Sutton the lady was taken ill and was obliged to leave the coach and stay at an inn with her husband. At Reigate the other two men left the coach to enquire after a friend. They quickly returned to inform the coachman that the friend had returned to London and, as he would not now be meeting them at Brighton, there was no point in their continuing their journey. The coachman and guard proceeded alone to Brighton where the theft was discovered. Presumably the money was now in the hands of the thieves in either Sutton or Reigate. Despite the offer of a £300 reward, the money, a huge sum in those days, was never recovered.

Banstead Downs, former home of the famous mutton provided by the sheep which grazed there, is less extensive an area than it used to be, and much that remains near the road is overgrown with scrub, but considerable open areas survive and valiant efforts are being made by volunteer groups and individuals to cut back the scrub and rescue parts of the famous Downs from extinction. Another milestone stands just south of the A217/A297 junction. New milestones, of which this is probably one, were placed along the road from Banstead Downs to Lowfield Heath in November 1830 as some of the old ones had been uprooted and others defaced – vandalism is not new! Sixteen stones were set out. They were made of Portland stone and were carted to the site and planted at a cost of £2.3s.6d each.

There is an open feel to the country south of Banstead Downs even though a lot of building development has taken place. This was a tract of heath and woodland, of which Burgh Heath is a considerable remnant. As with the Downs, much of the heathy woodland is covered by recent growth of scrub. In coaching times the land was much more open and kept that way by its use as common grazing.

Before Burgh Heath is reached, a road called Tangier Wood preserves the name of the Tangier Inn. This was a favourite stop for some coaches and, notably, was visited by George IV whenever he passed. An attraction for the king was a glass of "alderberry" wine served "roking hot" by the fair hands of the proprietor, Miss Jeal. This open and windswept hilltop area must have been a grim place in the winter, and warm refreshment doubly welcome. Miss Jeal's hospitable establishment has long gone but the pond at Burgh Heath still remains. This was the main source of water for livestock in the area and for some domestic uses also.

Tadworth toll gate lay at the southern end of Burgh Heath adjoining an area known, with some justification, as The Wilderness. The gate is shown on old maps just to the north of what is now Shelvers Way. Past the gate the road continues through Kingswood, past a milestone re-erected with an inaccurate alignment in the middle of the dual carriageway, and over a switchback road, now smoothed with embankments in the hollows. The whole region of heath and woodland that lay, and largely still lies, between Sutton and Reigate was described by Cobbett in "Rural Rides" as:

> "... about as villainous a tract as England contains. The soil is a mixture of gravel and clay, with big yellow stones in it, sure sign of really bad land."

The poor quality of the soil is, no doubt, the main reason for so much woodland in the district having survived the probing tentacles of suburbia. On a map of 1810 another toll gate, known as Walton Heath Gate, is shown north of Reigate Hill. A ticket bought in Sutton allowed passage through all the gates before the centre of Reigate.

Coach passengers approached Reigate Hill with some excitement, as this was one of the most significant places on the Classic route. The steep gradient of the road was much more difficult for coaches than the gaps through the North Downs, north of Godstone and along the Mole valley, so it was not the obvious route south. However, its use was well established because it was the link to London for the locally important town of Reigate.

At the top of the hill there is still a milestone surviving which gives distances to London, Sutton, Reigate and Brighton. Another milestone stands to the west of the road at the bottom of the hill. Between the two, Reigate Hill was always considered a major obstacle to the passage of coaches. It was one of the best-known, and indeed notorious, features on any of the roads to Brighton. It was subject to much engineering effort as the demands of coach traffic increased and a number of variations on the routes were tried in an effort to find the best way. One of these followed roughly the line of the present road, another went from Nutley Lane up Colley Hill to Walton Heath, a third track followed Wray Lane and a fourth alternative was by the track which leaves the main road where it bends at the bottom of the hill. This track, a narrow, sunken footpath today, is still marked at its southern end by a weather-beaten wooden sign saying *Public Highway*.

The old tracks would have been used by pedestrians and horses only. When travelling in the London direction, passengers in carriages would have to alight and walk up the hill, which was too steep for horses with a fully loaded coach. Shergold, quoted by Harper in *The Brighton Road*, suggests, with tongue in cheek, but perhaps also with some memory of reports of past events, that these occasions when passengers walked provided a novel situation on the journey and encouraged relaxation amongst the passengers. The more able would help those who had difficulty surmounting the hill, and this was the chance for a young man to offer his arm to an attractive young lady passenger in the hope of furthering their acquaintance. In Shergold's opinion, "It is said that matches are made in heaven; it may likewise be said that matches more often begin in the old stage-coaches, and that railroads are the antipodes of love."

The turnpike trustees first discussed improvements to the road between Reigate and Sutton at a meeting in the Swan Inn, Reigate on 15th April 1755, and work to improve Reigate Hill was quickly commenced. It progressed so well that the new road up the hill was opened in the spring of the following year. Tolls for maintenance were assured as the old alternative routes were then blocked off. Excavation of the chalk to cut the new road was a major undertaking, and the vicar of Reigate provided some local amusement by introducing his own brainchild for speeding up the process. He arranged for a huge battering ram to attack the chalk, apparently inspired by the biblical battering rams used against the walls of Jerusalem. The ram was so heavy that it took more than 20 men to operate it. Most of the people of Reigate turned out to watch, and termed the event 'Ram Fair'. On the following day, just two men with picks and shovels managed to shift more chalk than the ram and its 20 operators had achieved and so the vicar's scheme was abandoned.

In 1824 further work created a deep cutting through the upper part of the hill, and this was spanned by a suspension bridge the following year. This cut enabled the road to avoid a sharp bend at the top of the hill where the road had swung round to join the top of Wray Lane, a line occupied by the present car park. However from either direction the passage of Reigate Hill was always an event to be remembered. Coaches heading south through the cutting did not have to struggle up the steep gradient but had the daunting task of descending it safely; then they were suddenly confronted with extensive views across the Weald. According to Harper:

> "... the suddenness of it makes the stranger gasp with astonishment; the beauty of that wonderful view from the very rim and edge of the hill compels his admiration. It is the climax up to which he has been toiling all those long, ascending gradients from Sutton; and it is worth the toil."

Henry Wigstead, writing a century earlier, in 1789, spoke of the:

> "... delightful prospect of the South Downs in Sussex. But near the road, (which is scoop'd out of the hill,) the Declivity is so steep and abrupt, that the Spectator cannot help being struck with Terror though softened by Admiration."

The view can still be enjoyed today by standing in the car park where the old road once ran. One can still see the "delightful prospect of the South Downs" but parts of the nearer view are much obscured by the trees which now cover most of what was open grassland in coaching days. Perhaps because of this it is unlikely that modern observers are "struck by terror" at the steepness of the declivity. It is easy to imagine, however, that descent of this hill would have been an alarming experience for passengers perched high on the roof of a swaying coach, largely relying on the strength of a team of horses for their safety. A runaway coach here would have been fatal. Now, cars speed up and down the hill with little diminution of speed apart from that occasioned by traffic jams. Probably most of the drivers are unaware that they have been on a significant hill at all. Trees have not only covered the grassy slopes but they also conceal vast hollows carved out of the chalk to provide material for lime works. These quarries were cut to the west of the road and, in the days of coaching, would have presented gleaming white cliffs at the base of the hill.

James Pollard produced many fine prints of the activity on the roads in coaching's Golden Age. One of these depicts a well-laden stage coach pulling up to the toll gate at the bottom of Reigate Hill. It shows a good strong team with the whole equipage moving well, but undoubtedly some, if not all, of the passengers shown on the print would have had to alight and walk after the coach reached the gate. The road surface is good, but dust rises from it and there are shallow ruts, a reminder that, even on the best roads, no coach could help swaying as it was pulled along.

This toll gate stood at the bottom of the hill, near where the Yew Tree public house now stands and, earlier, there was another toll gate just before the road turned to go around Castle Rock. The circuit of the rock is still followed by the present road, although traffic is now only one way. It follows the line of the High Street and then turns south down Bell Street. At the same time that the cutting was being made, at the top of Reigate Hill work was put in hand to avoid this short detour at the bottom. A tunnel was dug beneath Castle Rock so that the old route by the High Street need no longer be used. The tunnel was opened in 1824 and tolls were charged for its use: 6 pence for a coach and four, 3 pence for a coach and pair or a post chaise, and smaller amounts for single horses. It reduced the journey to Brighton by a quarter of a mile and was considered a great engineering feat. The tunnel survives, but now only for pedestrian use.

The diarist Fanny Burney travelled through Reigate with the Thrale family and said of the town that "it is a very old, half ruined borough". She did, however, acknowledge that Reigate Hill afforded a "fine prospect". The town cannot have been as bad as Miss Burney's condemnation implies, as it was a popular coaching stop for many travellers. It was the last town of any significant size on this route before the coach reached Brighton and was well equipped to look after coaches.

There were two main coaching inns in Reigate, but sadly neither of them is still standing today. They were the Swan, near the eastern end of the High Street, and the White Hart at the top of Bell Street. The Prince Regent had a suite of rooms reserved for him at the White Hart which he frequently used when on his way to Brighton. Many coaches made a customary lunch stop at one or other of these inns. This, like many meals at coaching inns, was frequently yet another rushed meal. Some coaches, however, made a point of stopping for longer in Reigate so that the passengers had time to visit the Barons' Cave beneath the ruins of Reigate Castle, a cave where the barons are supposed, erroneously, to have gathered before meeting King John at Runnymeade.

Just as the design of coaches gradually changed and the coachmen themselves improved in skill and demeanour, so too was there, by the start of the nineteenth century, the appearance of a new breed of coachman. With the arrival of the nineteenth century both roads and coaches had improved to such an extent that it became fashionable for gentlemen to drive a coach – that is to say, the stage coach itself, rather than the gentleman's own carriage. The fashion spread through all the major routes of the country but had its origin on the Brighton road. The participants were usually sporting gentlemen, some driving a coach for enjoyment, when good weather and inclination tempted them. Others were Corinthians, young profligate noblemen, brought near to ruin by their reckless lifestyle, who chose to drive a coach out of necessity as well as for pleasure.

Some of the gentlemen dressed like a professional coachman and took a delight in acting the part throughout their journey. Of these, some were betrayed by their poor driving. Others were not only good drivers but went to considerable pains to keep up the pretence of being real coachmen. Such was the Marquis of Worcester who drove the *Beaufort* coach. He was a fine coachman who would even accept a tip from a passenger to maintain the illusion. Another was the Hon. Fred Jerningham, who drove the *Brighton Day Mail*. W. Outram Tristram wrote about them in 1893 and states that they were "artists to the tips of their fingers, who never solicited fees, and yet pocketed them when offered, with as much readiness and relish as could be shown by the poorest 'knights of the whips'".

Of all the Brighton road amateurs, however, the most notable were undoubtedly the drivers of the *Age*. The first of these was Harry Stevenson, an Old Etonian and Cambridge graduate. The *Age* was his second coach and, although we are told he was penniless, like so many of the amateurs he cannot have been truly so as the *Age* was built specially for him by Aldebert, the leading coach builder of the period. Stevenson's ambition was to be the finest driver of the finest coach on the Brighton road; an ambition to be fully realised.

He first appeared in Brighton in 1827, fresh from Cambridge and already an expert driver. For a short time he drove for another Brighton coachmaster, but in 1828 he put the *Age* on the road. The *Age* outshone all rivals for elegance and comfort. The coach itself was coloured blue and silver, and instead of brass on the harness it was silver-plated. The horse cloths were edged with deep silver lace and gold thread and embroidered in each corner with a crown and a spray of laurel.

Instead of a guard, Stevenson employed a liveried servant who, during stops for a change of horses, handed round a silver box of sandwiches and glasses of excellent sherry. It is said that he "always remembered the social graces of his birth and was singularly refined and courteous". If the coach was the finest so was its driver. Viator Junior, a contemporary commentator on coaching, wrote:

> "I am not aware if, to quote a vulgar saying, he was born with a silver spoon in his mouth, but I certainly think he must have been brought into

> the world with a whip and reins in his hand, for in point of ease and elegance of execution as a light coachman he beats nineteen out of twenty of the regular working dragsmen into fits, and as an amateur is only to be approached by two or three of the chosen few."

He may not have been penniless, but to maintain his coach in such a way must have been a considerable drain on his resources. However, his illustrious career was terminated abruptly. He died, aged 26, from an illness that may perhaps have been the result of an accident. Mountfield quotes his last words:

> "He became delirious and had to be tied down to his bed. When he grew weak the restraining bands were removed, and he struggled to sit up, holding himself as if once more upon the box of the *Age*. 'Let them go George; I have them,' he suddenly cried, then fell back exhausted and never spoke again."

The *Age* remained on the Brighton road and was later driven by another remarkable amateur driver, Sir St. Vincent Cotton, a Cambridgeshire baronet. He was so much addicted to gambling that he is said to have lost two fortunes at the gaming table. A gambling incident told of him refers to an occasion when some friends and he were cracking nuts after dinner when they found that some contained maggots, and so a maggot race was suggested. The maggots were lined up on the table and encouraged to race by being pricked with needles to spur them on. Sir St. Vincent's took the lead and betting took place with great excitement, and the pricking of maggots increased in fury. At this point one maggot, previously considered a complete outsider, crept up close to Sir St. Vincent's leader. The baronet was certain to either win or lose heavily and unfortunately pricked his maggot too deeply so that it curled up and died. The outsider passed by and won! Sir St. Vincent lost £30,000 on the occasion but subsequently came into a third fortune and settled down. While very short of money he drove the *Age* on the Brighton road for several years and so was able to earn his living while enjoying his sport, and enjoyed a reputation as a prince of whips. He was said to look very sharply after the half-crowns expected as gratuities.

A road where such amateur coachmen could flourish was indeed unique to its age. Its character has been eloquently recorded by W. Outram Tristram, who wrote in 1893 when most road traffic was still horse-drawn. He was an enthusiastic raconteur of the Golden Age of coaching, including coaching on the Brighton road, and clearly drew on personal memories as well as tales from the many others he had met on the road:

> "A peculiar flavour of the Regency lingers about the record of the Brighton road. It is a record, as I read it, with stupendous stocks, and hats with brims weirdly curly, casting deathly glances at lone maidens perambulating haplessly by the wayside; a record of 'The Fancy', as I see it drawn for me in the classic pages of Boxiana – thronging in their thousands, and in almost as many different kinds of conveyances to witness one of the many great battles decided on Crawley Down or Blindley Heath; a record finally of the great George himself, repairing to the health resort which his royal penetration had discovered, and repairing there in a coach and four, driven by his own royal hands, at the rate of fifty six round miles in four hours and a half."

The Tristram essence of the Brighton road was not just the refined nobility and gentry proceeding in a stately carriage to take up a fashionable lodging in Brighton. He speaks more of that part of the nobility, young and virile, old and coarse, who followed the call of excitement and sport down the line of the road:

> "Regent and emperor putting up at a wayside inn to witness a fight for the championship! Young sprigs chaunting and swiping till they dropped off their perches! The swells in their barouches and four hurrying from the metropolis! The noblemen and foreigners of

> rank crowding round the twenty-four foot ring! What can give us a better idea of the Brighton road in its prime than these facts? What paint more vividly what I call its 'Regency flavour', its slang, its coarseness, its virility – in a word, its Corinthianism?"

Reigate was always a bustle with coaching traffic which, after calling at one of the main inns, went down the slope of Bell Street and past the wall of Priory Park. Beside this wall, 150 years ago, there passed many a private carriage, stage coach and mail, all heading for that new and exciting town by the sea, Brighton. The park was private in those days, of course. Now it has been given to the people of Reigate for their enjoyment, a wonderful amenity for the town. The road soon rises again to surmount Cockshot Hill. This was a steep pull and the top has been lowered, originally to ease the passage of coaches.

Down Cockshot Hill, also quite a steep gradient, and the Woodhatch gate was reached. This stood south of the road junction near the Angel Inn, which still looks across the green today. The spot retains something of the ambience of coaching days. The inn itself has some venerable old beams and is clearly a worthy survivor from the coaching age. The road which turns off to the south-east here provided a useful alternative route south from Reigate once other new roads had been built. It linked with the new way to Povey Cross, and to the road past Horley. The Pentridge Wood toll gate stood on this road where it turns directly south.

The road between Reigate and Crawley is significant because it still follows the line of the very first new road to be made in Surrey; a turnpike made after an Act of 1690. This was, of course, well before the time of most turnpike Acts but even then it was clear that something had to be done. The ten miles to Crawley are particularly low-lying and marshy and a bank, referred to on a map of 1713 as the Old Causeway, was used for crossing the wet area. This bank had deteriorated so much over the years that the road was frequently impassable. The new road was essentially an improvement on the old causeway and, as described in Chapter 5, posts were put across each end. These posts remained in place until 1755 when they were removed and the road made open for coaches.

Between Woodhatch and Doversgreen the modern road still runs along a low embankment with drainage ditches on either side.

Before Doversgreen a milestone on the west side of the road is the first of a series made of sandstone and set at an angle to the road with directions to Brighton and Crawley on one side, London and Reigate on the other. Distances are given in miles and eighths of a mile.

The river Mole has to be crossed at Sidlow Bridge where it is cut deeply into the surrounding landscape. The modern bridge is high above river level but there must, in the past, have been a lower level bridge. After crossing the river the road continues south across more damp land and passes three more milestones. These stones are not in the original positions, but were moved to what was then a new section of road built in 1816. They were moved from the original road, which ran west in a wide loop over Horse Hills and now remains as a quiet lane. The present Horse Hills Farm was once the site of the Black Horse public house, and it had a toll gate beside it. Part of the old Black Horse survives behind the later farmhouse. A new Black Horse was built beside the new road after 1816. Better road building techniques had now made it possible to make a road across the wet lands, and a report at the time describes the old way as:

> "... circuitous and there divers Hills on Parts thereof."

The new road was:

> "... to fall in with the present turnpike road at Povey Cross. Thereby rendering the intercourse between the Metropolis and Sea Coast more speedy, particularly in the supply of Fish in the Mackeral and Herring season."

I am sure the good people of London appreciated their more reliable supply of mackerel and herring! Does any of this come from Brighton today?

Povey Cross is the place where the old coach road now comes to a halt at the edge of Gatwick Airport. This was a remote and rural spot marked by a milestone which has ended its days, for some unknown reason, at Ditchling Museum, many miles away. The old road continues a short distance beyond Povey Cross and then stops abruptly at the boundary fence of the airport.

The headwaters of the River Mole have their origins in the Gatwick area and the coach road crossed many small streams down the east side of Lowfield Heath. The airport now lies over all and the engineers who built it must have had a difficult task draining such a low-lying area. Now the former streams are drainage ditches, or else run in culverts underground. The natural wetness of the area is obvious from ditches beside the road which may frequently be seen full of water. The wetness, however, is nothing to what it was a century ago. Harper reports roads over Lowfield Heath being under four feet of water in February 1897 and further floods which, in October 1891:

> "... following upon a wet summer and autumnal weeks of rain, swelled the countless arteries of the Mole, and the highways became rushing torrents. Along the nut-brown flood floated the remaining apples from drowned orchards, with trees, bushes and hurdles."

Between Lowfield Heath and Crawley a great oak tree used to stand on the eastern side of the road and was recognised as the boundary mark between the counties of Surrey and Sussex. It was known as the County Oak and was felled in the 1840s. The tree is now remembered in the name of an out-of-town shopping area. Harper tells us that wood from the oak was used to make the screen in St. Margaret's Church, Ifield.

Crawley is an old settlement which stretched for about a mile along the road on the western side of the modern new town. As the Sun inn is at the northern end and the Half Moon at the other, a favourite joke of coachmen was to ask why Crawley was the longest town in the world and then point out these two inns. Crawley therefore stretches from the sun to the moon! The Sun is, however, further north than it used to be, having been moved to its present site, formerly a farm, from near the Crawley toll gate. This was sited at the north end of the High Street, somewhere under what is now the roundabout at the junction with Ifield Avenue. Crawley did not gain high favour with some writers of the coaching age. Shergold wrote that in 1801:

> "We soon arrived at Crawley, a miserable place, the sight of which always gave me, and many other persons whom I could mention, were it necessary to do so, the stomach ache."

Wigstead recorded "not meeting anything here particularly worthy of notice" when he visited in 1789. Rowlandson's drawing, executed at the same time, certainly shows a very rural scene, but it is not unattractive and it depicts the George inn which was surely always worthy of the notice of travellers. Opposite the George, the White Hart was built in 1770 as a new inn with extensive stabling to cater for the growing coach traffic, but the George was always Crawley's premier inn. The comments above seem very unfair when we consider the importance of inns to coach passengers. The quality of hospitality at the George did, however, vary over the years. Dench, landlord in the 1770s, was well known for providing good food, as was his brother who ran the Talbot in Cuckfield. His successor, Anscombe, did not do so well, and one writer referred to the inn during Anscombe's tenure as "a bad inn". The successful survival of this fine inn proves that the skills of Dench have been maintained over the years rather than those of Anscombe.

The tile-hung and beamed exterior of the George, and the arch through which coaches could pass to the yard and buildings behind, are typical of many old coaching inns. However, only the central part facing the High Street is from that time. The inn has later been extended on either side. Another pleasing feature, which has much more in common with the past than now, is the gallows sign outside, which is positioned to span the road beneath. In Crawley it crosses only part of the wider, modern road but most such signs have been removed completely as they succumb to the demands of modern road layouts. The sign is shown in Rowlandson's sketch, but the ravages of time necessitated replacement. The present sign dates from 1934. Inside, the George is equally attractive with a fine fireplace and heavy beams. It is certainly not difficult to envisage it as a thriving place in coaching days and, indeed, it has retained the welcoming feel of a successful inn.

A fascinating story related about the George is that the place has a ghost. A story displayed at the inn tells how those who broke their journey overnight may have felt more secure in their beds because a night watchman, Mark Heuston, six feet six inches in height and weighing 18 stone, was employed to patrol the corridors armed with cutlass and pistol. Unfortunately he would often neglect his duty and go to sleep in the broom cupboard opposite Room 7. While he slept, rooms were raided by a thief who took money and valuables and also ate the remains of suppers left in the rooms. It was decided to end this undesirable situation by setting a trap for the thief, and accordingly poison was added to wine left in the rooms. However, Heuston was not told of this. The day after the poison had been added, Heuston was found dead but it was never known whether he had really been the thief or if he had just been unfortunate in feeling thirsty on that particular night. In fairness to Heuston, he was allowed to drink leftover wine as one of his perks. The story is not forgotten because, to this day, footsteps, said to be those of Heuston, can be heard along the corridors at night and guests have reported "an uneasy feeling". The broom cupboard door may be found swinging open, even when it had been previously locked, and doors to bedrooms in the old part of the inn may be opened and closed as if the watchman is still walking the corridors, guarding the guests or looking for his wine.

The George is known to have been a staging point for contraband en route from the coast to London, and so the oldest parts of the inn must have been known to smugglers. Many respectable people also stayed there including the Prince of Wales, Charles James Fox and Richard Brinsley Sheriden. Many additions were made to the inn at this time, and assembly rooms were added at the rear. Perhaps less respectable, but certainly associating with the aristocracy, were prize fighters, many of whom spent the night at the George with their supporters before attending bouts at Crawley Down.

The roads followed by the prize fighting enthusiasts were, of course, routes also used by stage coaches. However, the preferred conveyances to the fight were private vehicles. Indeed, as today, those who could afford to do so would generally choose to drive themselves from London to Brighton. Anyone living beside the road would have seen an amazing variety of vehicles passing. The coaches, stage and mail, were the public transport of the day. At the other end of the scale were carriers, wagons and farm carts, and between the two were a multitude of private vehicles. A description of all these many different carriages would fill a book on its own, but the story of the Brighton roads would be incomplete without an acknowledgement of them. A detailed account by John Copeland in *Roads and their Traffic* provides a valuable source for much of the following summary.

If sporting young men had wished to drive a four-wheeled vehicle they would probably have chosen a phaeton. There were many different types of these but they were alike in having a seat perched up above the wheels which were, themselves, some four or five feet in diameter. The whole precarious equipage looked very stylish and could be pulled by a team of two, four or even six horses. The best models would incorporate all the latest technical innovations such as improved elliptical springs. The most expensive were built to order and fitted out to the particular specifications of the purchaser, with the best quality wood and leather, carved, painted and polished to perfection. Copeland quotes an example of a top-of-the-range phaeton being sold for £225. This, like the more expensive sports coupe cars today, was beyond the reach of most people but a cheaper, less expensively finished, version could be bought for under £50.

The equivalent of the sports car or smaller sporty hatchback was to be found amongst the great range of two-wheeled vehicles pulled by a pair of horses. Two types, which were very popular and fashionable with the aristocracy, were the curricle, driven uniquely by a pair of horses abreast, and the cabriolet, drawn by a single horse. Both these vehicles, but the cabriolet in particular, could have a small groom, a 'tiger', perched up on a seat at the back.

Gigs were used by many people and varied considerably around a basic two-wheeled design. The Whiskey was an improved design; a one-horse gig that 'whisked' the driver along. Other types were the Tilbury and the Stanhope. A gig with a hood to protect the driver from the weather was known as a Buggy. The popularity of the gig can be seen from the fact that more than a hundred gigs were counted passing through Croydon on their way to a prize fight at Crawley Down on 14th May 1819.

These small vehicles were driven by the owner and, like a sports car, had limited luggage capacity which made them unsuitable for long journeys. Luggage could, however, easily be carried by the other main type of vehicle on the road: the private carriage, many of which would pass down the Brighton roads every day, driven by the coachman employed by the families who owned them. Some had four seats inside, some two. As the art of coach building developed, they were often fitted out with great luxury and designed to match the elegance of their owner. As with modern motor cars they varied greatly in price and style. Landaus, barouches and broughams were particularly elegant, while fourgons and drags were rather more sober. A basic price for a carriage was over £100, although with extra fittings, the cost could rise to over twice as much. There was, of course, a thriving market in secondhand carriages. Copeland gives an example of an auction in Brighton in 1842 where a barouche "lined with purple cloth", and having driving and luggage boxes and patent lamps, was described as "nearly equal to new", and fetched £130. At the same auction another barouche fetched £100 and a cabriolet went for just £15.

It must be remembered that, for most people, the cost of owning and maintaining a carriage was prohibitive. Some could afford to travel with a hired post chaise, but most would use the stage or, possibly, the mail.

Plate 30

The Old Cock at Sutton in 1790, looking south. One of the best-known inns on the routes to Brighton, and particularly famous during the years when the landlord was 'Gentleman' Jackson, the former champion pugilist.

Plate 31

The view from the top of Reigate Hill. The "steep declivity" is much more masked by trees than in coaching days, but is still impressive.

Plate 32

Reigate old toll house. The open nature of the landscape made the steep scarp of the North Downs even more impressive.

Plate 33

The Yew Tree public house on Reigate Hill has now stood for many years on the site of the old toll house.

Plate 34

The *Comet* approaching Reigate Hill. This coach was operated by the great coach proprietor William Chaplin. The hill was a major obstacle on the most direct route between London and Brighton. The passengers here will probably have to get off at the toll gate and walk up the hill.

Plate 35

The old toll cottage, the site of which is now occupied by a roundabout at the north end of the High Street in Crawley.

Plate 36

The George, Crawley; a famous coaching inn and a favourite stop for coaches. One of the few where a 'gallows' sign still crosses part of the road outside.

Chapter 9
The 'Classic' Route: Crawley to Brighton

The road south from Crawley was thickly forested in coaching days, and large parts still remain of Tilgate Forest which was entered on passing through Pease Pottage gate. Both ends of the coach road through Pease Pottage are now closed off, leaving the village green a quieter place but with little of coaching interest.

The forest roads around Handcross were said to be haunted by two different ghosts. One was particularly involved with turnpike gates, playing tricks with bolts and bars and scaring the pike keepers. The other, also harmless, was nevertheless a much more frightening spectre. He was the ghost of 'Squire Powlett', an ex-guardsman who lived in St. Leonard's Forest and died in 1746. This ghost had no head and would spring up behind horsemen and ride with them as far as the forest boundary.

Handcross is not a particularly large settlement but is a pleasant place as the modern A23 takes traffic around the village. It used to be an important stopping place for the coaches on the Brighton road. There was a toll gate at the north end of the village, and one of a row of cottages there is called Tollgate Cottage. At the other end of the village is the reason why Handcross was important to coaches: the Red Lion. Sadly, the famous old inn was destroyed in a fire in 1978. A new Red Lion has been built on the same site and a photograph of its predecessor may be seen in the bar. It was widely believed in coaching times that the excellence of the drinks served at the Red Lion owed much to an agreement between the landlord and smugglers.

In the early years of the nineteenth century the main Brighton transport was by two-horse coaches, which made very slow progress. They travelled at only about four and a half miles an hour and spent a long time at each stop. So long was frequently spent at

Cuckfield that the passengers from Brighton would often choose to walk ahead and await the arrival of the coach at Handcross. This walk, a distance of over four miles, was quite tiring, but benches were provided outside the Red Lion, and Bannister the landlord:

> "... would walk forth from his inn, carrying a gallon bottle of gin in one hand and a small wicker basket of slices of gingerbread in the other. 'You must be tired gentlemen,' said he, 'come, take a glass and a slice.'"

The way between Handcross and Cuckfield is one of the most attractive stretches remaining of the old coach road. Even this comparatively unspoilt route has, however, undergone minor realignments over the years and, in places, the original route is marked by an overgrown and marshy hollow beside the present road. There are lovely views across the Sussex countryside and, beside the road, big old oak trees whose branches will surely have brushed the roofs of passing coaches. After a while the trees give way to the wide grassy expanse of Staplefield Common. Here stands the Jolly Tanners inn, which was an especially welcome sight to coach travellers as they could look forward to the speciality of the house: an excellent rabbit pie. So good was this that many a coach was delayed for up to two hours while the pie was being enjoyed. One of those who was happy to delay at this pleasant place was said to be none other than the Prince of Wales himself. Clearly the demand for speed on the journey could sometimes be subordinated to more immediately attractive claims on the passengers' time. Outside the inn there used to grow some large cherry trees. Cherry tart could follow the rabbit pie and the cherries, 'black-hearts', became famous. Coaches would stop under the trees when the cherries were in season and the outside passengers would help themselves to the fruit while they waited. The original trees have long since gone but a tree in the inn garden is said to be a descendant of those same 'black-hearts' of the old days.

The road continues gently southwards and, where it turns to the east at Slough Green, there was another toll gate, soon after which coaches entered Cuckfield. Much of the old centre of this small town has changed little since the days when coaches stopped there, partly because the railway avoided the town and went instead through what was then open country at neighbouring Haywards Heath. By the start of the nineteenth century 50 stage coaches a day were passing through Cuckfield and stopping at the inns there. There are no difficult corners in Cuckfield, yet in 1819, the *Coburg* coach was overturned here. It is hardly surprising that an overturn occurred because the coach was grossly top-heavy on that occasion, with 11 outside passengers crowded onto the roof at the same time. All of them were hurt and one subsequently died. The town remained important for coaches and was a favourite stop for the Prince of Wales, who came to know well the landlord of the King's Head, Daniel Dench, the brother of the landlord of the George in Crawley. A leaflet available at the inn includes a description written by Dench's daughter, of how she remembered it from her childhood:

> "My father was host of the King's Head which stood where Mr. Langton's house now is, and many is the royal guest the old inn welcomed. The Prince of Wales was a constant visitor, for he often drove from London to Brighton in a carriage and four, attended by two outriders and a second carriage and four in which were his pages, and the horses were changed at our house. He was very friendly with my father and knew all the postillions. We didn't like the outriders very much for many of them could not ride a bit and we were obliged to give them some of our best horses which were sometimes spoilt in consequence."

The King's Head was an important stop for coaches and maintained extensive stables. The original site was on the corner of Ockenden Lane from which it was moved into the present building in about 1840. In the King's Head there used to be a 'Parliament Clock' which was placed there after an Act of Parliament decreed that clocks must be visible at staging posts. The clock is now preserved at Queen's Hall, Cuckfield. It was made locally in 1797 and is unglazed so that no reflection from the glass could hide the time from a traveller looking in through the window. It is perhaps as well that the original King's Head no longer exists because the old inn had a ghost: that of a screaming chamber maid, covered in blood. The story goes that she was made pregnant by the landlord who subsequently got rid of her embarrassing presence by dropping a large geranium pot on her head from a great height. This may or may not have been an accident, although it was subsequently accepted as such.

Cuckfield museum preserves a bill issued by Daniel Dench, and also an advertisement for the other coaching inn of Cuckfield, the Talbot. This was formerly a small alehouse but was enlarged, and upgraded in name from the Hound to the Talbot around 1800. It was rebuilt in the 1820s and still stands, with a barn behind it where horses used to be stabled.

There are two old coach roads south from Cuckfield. One is now the A273 which passed through a toll gate at Butlers Green. The other ran through Ansty, where there are still some attractive old buildings and where, at the road junction, another toll gate stood. The two roads come together to cross the Adur, north of Burgess Hill. The present road to Ansty now runs in a cutting made to reduce the gradient and there are some fine old oak trees along it. Both these roads pass through some delightful countryside. It deserves a far better description than that given by Fanny Burney, who could only write that the view south towards the Downs from Cuckfield is "very curious and singular". Coach passengers must have enjoyed the view of the Downs, if only because it meant they were getting nearer to Brighton. Passengers travelling north would have seen the church spire of Cuckfield ahead of them; a welcome sight to those looking forward to the hospitality of the King's Head. South of Ansty there are more fine oak trees, and the former course of the coach road can be seen as a broad ditch beside the present highway.

The river Adur is crossed south of Ansty on a bridge which is, today, about 15 feet above river level. The Adur is about ten feet wide at this point and so carries a considerable amount of water even with normal flows. It must have been a worrying point of the coach journey in times of flood.

Soon after crossing the river, Burgess Hill appears, an uninteresting sprawl of buildings that came into existence with the arrival of the railway and the enclosure of St. John's Common in the first half of the nineteenth century. In coaching times this was all open heathland with very few buildings and a reputation as the haunt of smugglers who made use of the lonely heaths to hide their contraband.

A very pretty stream is crossed near New Close Farm and Friar's Oak. The inn here has been rebuilt in place of one that was well known in coaching times. Another sprawl of buildings soon appears: Hassocks and Keymer. As with Burgess Hill there were few houses here in the days when coaches passed, but fields lay in place of heathland and amongst them stood the lonely Stone Pound gate. The old gate area, at the A237/B2116 crossroads, is now all built up, a lonely area no longer.

The passage of Stone Pound gate meant that another of the major obstacles on the Brighton road was shortly to be encountered by the coaches. The high scarp of the South Downs looms from east to west across the way and its presence meant that Clayton Hill had to be climbed. Like Reigate Hill, this was a place for passengers to get out and walk. The steepness is such that nervous passengers probably preferred to trust their own legs rather than the horses. On a good day the view from the top is impressive. To the north lies a patchwork of fields, farms and villages, while from the summit is a first glimpse of Brighton and the sea. The views, and the slopes of the Downs themselves, have inevitably been commented on by many travellers. The prosaic Wigstead, in 1789, could only comment that the South Downs "are generally covered with sheep, remarkable for the fineness of their wool". A century later Harper wrote much more lyrically:

> "From the summit of the Downs the Weald is seen, spread out like a pictorial map, the little houses, the little trees, the ribbon-like roads looking like dainty models; the tiny trains moving out of Noah's Ark stations and vehicles crawling the highways like objects in a miniature land of make-believe. Looking southward, Brighton is seen – a pillar of smoke by day, a glowing, twinkling light at evening; but for all it is so near, it has very little affected the old pastoral country life of the downland villages. The shepherds, carrying as of yore their Pyecombe crooks, still tend huge flocks of sheep, and the dull and hollow music of the

sheep-bells remains as ever the characteristic sound of the district. Next year the sheep will be shorn, just as they were when the Saxon churls worked for their Norman masters, and, unless a cataclysm of nature happens, they will continue so to be shorn centuries hence."

Harper's assurance that little would change was not entirely justified. Even in his own day he lamented the decline of sheep-shearing songs which used to be sung when the shepherds gathered together. He would certainly be astonished today to see many of the fields used for horses and large areas of former sheep pasture sown with crops. Fortunately there are many sheep still to be seen grazing the downland turf, but they are not the only use of the hills as of old. The once famous Pyecombe crooks with their elaborately curled heads are no longer in evidence and the "dull and hollow music of the sheep bells" has ceased. The change is due to economic and social factors, which have had consequences beyond anything Harper could foresee, rather than to any cataclysm of nature as he surmised. Seen from the Downs, Brighton still has twinkling lights; far more than in the past, but clean air legislation has removed the daytime view of a great pillar of smoke.

Other aspects of the scenery that have survived the passage of time are the dew ponds, the only water supply for the flocks of old, and also the windmills, Jack and Jill, that crown the Downs near the top of the hill. Of the shepherds there are few to be seen on the Downs nowadays and, when they are encountered, they lack the picturesque quality of their predecessors. A good impression of how the old shepherds looked may, however, be gathered from the collection of shepherd's equipment on display in Cuckfield museum. The linen smock is made of heavy material, more like canvas than linen as we would think of it. It is a magnificent garment and would have given excellent protection against the weather. There is also a large umbrella, made from the same heavy stuff. In addition is a pair of boots, a fine crook and a number of other tools. Clothes had to be strong and serviceable on these open hills where shelter is scarce and winter winds can be biting cold. A present-day shepherd who was having a bite to eat beside his Land Rover agreed that he had a fine job on a sunny day but claimed, with feeling, that when it is necessary to be on the Downs in bad wintry weather, shepherding in

Sussex is as hard as anywhere in the country. At such times the open landscape is exposed to every wind that blows and can be bleak indeed.

The Clayton Hill road was deeply cut into the chalk in order to reduce its gradient but, like Reigate Hill on the North Downs, it still remained a formidable obstacle for a laden coach. Amongst nervous passengers there must always have been some fear that the coach would get out of control when descending the hill, careering downwards to inevitable destruction. Even if they were reassured by the guard's deft use of the skid, their ears must have suffered. One writer comments on how the skid would scream and grumble as metal tyres contacted the metal shoe and it was ground into the rocky surface of the road.

When travelling uphill the passengers were out of danger from the coach but had to exert themselves more when they were obliged to leave the vehicle and walk. To modern eyes it would have been amusing to observe the distinction maintained between the 'gentlefolk' who occupied inside seats and the lesser mortals on the roof. To quote Harper:

> "Going up-hill one walked, to ease the horses, insides and outsides then equal; the insides, greatly condescending, holding converse with the occupants of the roof, always, however, with the strict understanding – no less strict if not mentioned – that this gracious act must not be taken advantage of by those outsiders claiming acquaintance when the coach stopped at the inns, where this all-important difference in caste was recognised by distinct eating apartments being provided."

The top of the Downs could be particularly bleak but the horses, coachmen and outside passengers were exposed to the weather wherever they were on the journey, and of all the weather they met the most dramatic struggles were concerned with snow. Coachmen knew nothing of gritting lorries and a four-horse coach meant a power unit of just four horse power. Furthermore, horses are not mechanical and can shy away from the weather and slip on a treacherous surface. There were times when the efforts of coachmen and their teams to complete their journeys were little short of heroic, and those who wrote about them recorded their feats with admiration.

The deep snow that affected the Lewes road in 1789 has already been mentioned. Two other particular snowstorms that occurred during the coaching period, above all the rest to affect the Brighton road, were of such severity that records of them have come down to us. Fortunately neither occasioned loss of life, unlike a storm in 1806 when the guard on the Bristol mail was frozen to death, but both tested the endurance of coachmen and guards to the limit.

Bishop quotes a local report of a coach in the exceptional winter of 1808:

> "On February 12th, 1808, the coaches to London were unable, for the first time within memory, to proceed on their journey, by reason of the snow, and all had to return after going a short distance. Mr. Pattenden, in driving his post-coach over the Downs, by the Devil's dyke, experienced the greatest difficulty in proceeding; though full inside and out, the wind was so high, that every moment it was expected the coach would be overturned. Then the frost was so severe, that several passengers declared that they must have perished, had they not returned. An elderly man, named Bursbee, was totally deprive of feeling, and slipt from the top of the coach, unobserved by the other passengers, but missing him on their arrival at the coach office, a search was instituted and he was brought safely back. Had he remained on the hill but a short time longer he must inevitably have perished."

The most famous storm of all, and one which lived forever in the memories of those who experienced it, was the Great Snowstorm of Christmas 1836. Fortunately the cold was not too severe but the amount of snow was phenomenal. It started to fall over much of the country on Friday 23rd December, when the wind changed from south south-west to north north-east. The storm affected all the country, with the south being very hard hit, and snow continued to fall for nearly a week. On Christmas Eve, Saturday, there was already a lot of snow on the ground and the wind speed increased to gale force, continuing to blow throughout Christmas Day and with particular strength that evening. Snow was everywhere except on the hill tops from whence it was blown to lower-lying, more sheltered, areas. By midnight on Christmas Day it was breast high in many places and there are records of drifts over 30 feet deep. On Rose Hill in Brighton the depth was 15 feet and on many roads the depth was above the level of the roofs of coaches. Trees fell and hedgerows were obliterated so the vehicles that did try to get out would struggle through the drifts only to find that they had left the road and were stranded in the middle of fields.

Any travel was clearly impossible for almost everyone, but it is a tribute to the courage and determination of the mail coachmen and guards that they still tried manfully to carry out their duties. The Brighton mail which left London on Sunday when the storm was already raging must have been in the hands of men of iron because they had managed to reach the bottom of Clayton Hill, much of the journey already completed, before they became stuck. There was only one passenger and he stayed in the coach with the coachman while the guard, with a local man as his guide, carried the mailbags to Brighton on horseback. He reached the post office, half dead, at 1am on Monday having spent seven hours fighting his way through the snow to Brighton. At times the snow was so deep, and the footing so uncertain, that the horse, guard and mailbags all finished rolling in the snow. In the morning the coachman and passenger managed to turn the coach round and return to Friar's Oak. The coachman eventually reached Brighton at 4am on Tuesday.

The attempts to dispatch mail from Brighton to London were equally eventful. The mail left Brighton as usual at 10.30am on Sunday but about eight miles from the town, at the bottom of Clayton Hill, it fell into a hollow of drifted snow from which it could not be moved. The guard set off to get assistance but when he returned no trace could be seen of the coach, coachman or the three passengers, so deeply was the coach buried. When the coach was found it could not be pulled out from the hollow. The coachman, guard and passengers slept the night at Clayton, as the road further north was by now quite impassable. The following day the guard took the mails through to London on horseback. He finally arrived there on Tuesday night having been obliged to ride across fields in places in order to avoid drifts on the roads.

When the mail failed to arrive in Crawley, the postmaster there sent a man in a gig on Monday afternoon, to discover the cause. Nothing was heard for some hours so another man went on horseback to search and he eventually found the gig, horse and driver all buried in the snow and totally exhausted. Together they managed to turn the gig and so got back to Crawley. The man had found no tidings of the mail and, not unnaturally, refused to go out again.

No coaches at all left Brighton on the Monday, Boxing Day, but mail was sent by men on horseback who took five hours to reach Pyecombe and had to stay there all night. On Tuesday six men on foot continued with the bags. They got as far as Cuckfield after nine miles of extreme effort; then took horses to Crawley from where they hired a post chaise to London.

Modern traffic can still be disrupted by snow, and vehicles become stranded, but the drivers can now communicate with mobile phones and can expect help from the emergency services within a reasonable time. The old coaches were alone, stranded and with no means of summoning help other than on foot, yet they still managed to battle through, Above all, the mails had to be delivered, even though it be through deep drifts and done on horseback. Would our modern postal services react to adversity with such resolution?

The great snowstorm had affected so many people and given rise to so many newsworthy, and indeed heroic, incidents, that large numbers of prints were produced of subjects such as coaches battling through the snow, and inns surrounded by snowdrifts. These prints, and the memories associated with them, have had a lasting effect on the subject matter of Christmas cards and it is thought that this storm was the origin of the phrase 'a white Christmas'.

After climbing Clayton Hill, the coaches reached the small village of Pyecombe which seems to defy all logic in terms of where it is sited. It stands on a spur of land extending south from Wolstonbury Hill, on the waterless chalk and exposed to all the weather may throw at it. Yet, there it does stand, for centuries a centre for downland shepherds. The coach road passed close to the east side of the church down what is now only a narrow lane as the village is bypassed by the modern main roads. Despite the proximity of these roads, the place has preserved something of its old world atmosphere. The solidly built little church has a painting of the royal arms over the chancel arch, presumably painted by a local artist and dating from coaching days. The lion in the painting looks down on the congregation with an engaging grin. In that church generations of shepherds must have been baptised, married and finally laid to rest. The other centre for much of their lives was the Plough inn, which still stands at the southern end of the village and was in a good position to serve passing coaches as well as the local people. Now more of a restaurant than a pub, it still retains a friendly atmosphere which the shepherds of old would have known.

The road leaves Pycombe down a long and gentle descent to Brighton, but was a tiring pull for horses going in the other direction. It follows a dry valley, the sides of which rise gently on each side of the road. Soon Patcham is reached, where a toll gate was situated after being removed north from Preston in 1854. Patcham is well worth exploring but it hides its charms from the traffic of the modern main road. The way leading up the valley side from the Brighton road to Patcham church is a pretty place with a charming muddle of cottages that look as if they have naturally grown there. On the north side of the church is a memorial to Daniel Scales who was "unfortunately shot on Thursday evening Nov. 17th 1796". Much of the rest of the lettering is now obliterated but Harper reproduces the moral verse that was formerly engraved there. He also tells us that Scales was one of a gang of smugglers who, while coming from Brighton with smuggled goods, were confronted by excise men and soldiers at Patcham. Most of the gang ran off but Scales stood fast and refused to surrender his goods or himself. The excise man confronting him, knowing that Scales was a dangerous man, promptly shot him through the head.

From Patcham onwards, the way to Brighton is now urban but pleasantly softened by trees and ornamental parkland. Preston gate was probably situated where a wall extends out towards the road from the park wall. It was erected about 1807 but was replaced by a gate north of Withdean in 1854. In 1789 Preston was described as "a beautiful spot, adorned with a great number of venerable elms". Today these have given way to some fine old lime trees.

Coach accidents could occur, even on this gentle and well-maintained stretch of road. Coaches were subject to much wear and tear and so structural failure was not unlikely. In March 1836, at Patcham, the axel tree of the *Magnet* broke, which caused the horses to start. The coachman was thrown, and the coach wheels went over his leg and broke it. Another cause was bad driving, particularly because of the way some coachmen would race each other. On one such occasion, near Preston gate, the *Dart* tried to pass the *Phoenix*, crashed into it and overturned it. One passenger had his thigh bone broken and others were seriously injured. "The shrieks of the passengers were heartrending."

The elms of Preston cannot have been typical of the road into Brighton, as a characteristic of the area and of the town itself, which was remarked on by many visitors, was the treeless nature of the district. This was a result, presumably, of the importance of sheep grazing, which sacrificed trees in favour of downland grass. The lack of trees was an unenviable aspect of the town's reputation. Dr Johnson, visiting in 1770, declared that:

"... if one had in mind to hang one's self for desperation at being obliged to live there, it would be difficult to find a tree on which to fasten a rope."

Since that time fine trees have now grown to maturity in many parts and thus remedied the situation, and many people choose to live there without any sense of desperation at all. Another improvement in modern times is the quality of the air. Pollution is not a new phenomenon and, throughout the Victorian age and before, people became accustomed to the soot and grime of towns. Harper, in 1892, could say of the view from St. Nicholas' church:

"From here you can, with some trouble, catch just a glimpse of the watery horizon through the grey haze that rises from countless chimney-pots, and never a breeze but blows laden with the scent of soot and smoke."

Petrol-driven vehicles however, triumphant successors to the coaches of old, although not perhaps obstructing the view with their fumes, can harm the health of all in a manner of which the coaches, at least, were innocent.

The many fine Regency buildings in Brighton reflect the distinction bestowed on it by the builders of that period. One, however, intimately associated with the Regent himself, transcends all others: the Pavilion. It has been both admired and despised over the years, but never ignored. William Cobbett described it as "the pointed half of a large turnip on a board with four smaller ones at the corners". A more sycophantic description is in *Patterson's Roads*:

> "The pavillion, belonging to His Majesty, who has shown his superior taste by considerably enlarging and improving the building... His Majesty has, in the erection of the terrestrial paradise, placed on British ground the most original, unique, and perhaps magnificent structure in Europe."

The Pavilion is a mixture of various styles – Greek, Moorish and Russian – but, particularly inside, a Chinese influence pervades. Whatever one's opinion of the amazing edifice – and the modern age looks on it with more kindly eyes than did many of our predecessors – there is little doubt that it is the hub and the abiding memory of Brighton.

In coaching days Brighton had another hub. Almost under the Pavilion walls was the centre of operations for Brighton coaches: Castle Square. At the height of the coaching era six out of the seven coaching offices in Brighton were situated there. Of these the most important were the Blue Office and the Red Office. In the early nineteenth century the Blue Office was the base of Crossweller and Co. who ran "morning and night" coaches from Brighton to London. As the coaching age came to an end in 1839 five London coaches ran from the Blue Office operated by Strevens and Co. and five from the Red Office by Mr Goodman. Many other coaches ran from various inns in the vicinity of the square. When the first railway was built between London and Brighton, a total of 36 coaches ran between the two places every week. The average fare at this time was 21 shillings for insides and 12 shillings for outsides. The average journey time was six hours.

In the quiet area of Castle Square today, much rebuilt and quite unrecognisable as such a vibrant centre of the coaching age, it is hard to imagine the noise and activity of past years. The activity continued through all hours, but reached a crescendo when the Pavilion clock struck and signalled the departure of more coaches. Arrivals too presented a scene of great animation when, amongst the many other services, bathing women would present their cards to prospective customers. These ladies were advertising their bathing machines, covered carts which could be pulled into the sea. Customers could change in the enclosed interior and then be helped into the water by the attendant. John George Bishop, writing in 1880, but with clear memories of Brighton as it had been in the old days, gives a vivid description of the scene in Castle Square which deserves to be repeated here:

> "From early morn till late at night – from the bottom of North Street to the Steine – in olden times the Square was crowded with a motley, ever-changing throng of life, and was at times impassable... Groups of idlers... were to be seen around the various offices watching the arrival and departure of the coaches; and, mingled with these, were passengers hurrying to and fro to secure their places, followed by busy porters with luggage, boxes, &c. Cads and touters were here, there, and everywhere, on the look-out for a job. Cabs were constantly going to and from the Square, or busy setting-down or taking-up fares. At the doors of half-a-dozen offices at one time might be seen brightly-coloured coaches, horsed by splendid teams champing their bits or pawing the ground, as if entering into the excitement of the scene, and eager for the start. On some of the coaches were trimly attired, bright-coated guards, 'towering in their pride of place,' ever and anon playing their bugles... And then, when the start was about to take place, what redoubled excitement was there! When the passengers were at last seated; the luggage piled or stowed away; when the coachman had mounted the box, had tightened the "ribbons," and flourished his whip in conscious pride; and when, at a given signal, as the clock struck the hour from the old Pavillion tower, the horse-cloths were dexterously snatched away by the attendant ostlers, the guard struck up a familiar air on his bugle, and the words issued from many a mouth, 'Off she goes!' Altogether, it was a scene which one cannot

adequately describe, but which can never be forgotten by those old enough to have witnessed it."

Bishop records that, by 1880, even the buildings which had surrounded the Square in coaching days had been replaced by shops. It was, however, the demise of the pulsating life of the Square, as described above, that was the most striking and poignant change.

Many of the visitors drove their own carriages and stayed in the newly built fashionable houses, often hired for the season. Others may have stayed at the Ship Inn, with its elegant frontage, which still stands, although extended and much altered internally, facing the sea at the end of Ship Street. This inn was the Brighton terminus for some coaches, notably Batchelar's *New Machine* which provided the first direct service from London to Brighton. Not all of the visitors were of sufficient notability to be invited to a reception at the Pavilion, but other diversions were open to them. In particular, the sporting proclivities of many gentlemen were well catered for. Venues for prize fighting and cock fighting were made accessible by the road, and further attractions were available at Brighton itself. J. A. Erredge, writing in 1862, states that the Prince of Wales kept a pack of harriers there but the whole pack had to be destroyed when one dog exhibited signs of hydrophobia. The Duke of Richmond hunted fox hounds in the area, and two other packs were supported by subscription.

A handbill is reproduced by Erredge on another favourite sport:

COCKING
To be fought at the Cock Pit,
WHITE LION,
NORTH STREET, BRIGHTON,
ON
THURSDAY
THE 18TH APRIL, 1811
a Main of Cocks for twenty Guineas
a Battle, and Fifty Guineas the Main;
between the Gentlemen of the Isle of
Wight and the Gentlemen of Sussex.
Feeders {Pollard, Isle of Wight

{Holden, Sussex.
N.B.— A pair of cocks to be on the Pit at
Eleven o'clock.

The meeting on Easter Monday 1810 for cock fighting and badger baiting in a field beside the Bear public house on the Lewes road has already been referred to. On the following day it was traditional to have a bull bait at Hove but, as it was taking place, the bull broke away from its stake and charged the spectators, fortunately without anyone being seriously injured. The bait was postponed until June 11th when it was held with a dinner subsequently provided at the Ship Inn. Bull baiting was a very popular diversion and what we would consider a disgusting spectacle was said to give pleasure to all. The bull was tethered in a pen and dogs were set on to attack it, up to 30 dogs at one time. An award was given for the dog which gave the best performance. Dogs were often killed and the bull hurt so there was much blood for the spectators to 'enjoy'. The bull was seldom killed but was toured around to many venues and used many times. When such bulls were eventually killed, either by the dogs or simply through age and injuries, their meat was in much demand from housewives who claimed it had a superior flavour.

A less contentious diversion was to ride that precursor of the bicycle, a hobby horse. To quote Erredge:

> "About forty years since (i.e. the 1820s) 'hobby horse' exercise was a very favourite diversion with the gentry. These 'hobbies' were the original velocipedes, now worked by a crank action; but they then consisted only of a fore and hind wheel, with a slight saddle rail between, upon which the rider sat, holding on by the handle that guided the front wheel, and then, by striking out his feet with a walking action, the machine became propelled, its speed being regulated by the ability of the horseman. Much practice and great judgment were required to make a proficient rider. Many extraordinary feats of pedestrianism were performed with these machines; but the most arduous were the competing with the stage coaches to and from London."

The racecourse, still thriving today, provided sport with horses of a more conventional type.

Travellers took the coach to Brighton for many reasons, but the various sports were not the most important of them. Brighton had risen to importance due to the growth in popularity of sea bathing, and the attractions of the beach remain constant to the present day. Over two hundred years ago Wigstead was aware of one attraction which may still interest the male visitor to Brighton's beaches:

> "The number of beautiful Women, who every Morning court the Embraces of the Watery God, far exceeds that of any other Bathing Place in the Kingdom."

These "beautiful Women" were, no doubt, well shielded from prying eyes as they entered the sea from the cover of bathing machines, the tickets for which could be purchased from the ladies who operated the machines.

As might be expected, the press of traffic in Brighton made accidents on its streets inevitable. One of the worst occurred on July 15th 1833 at the south end of Gloucester Place. The *Quicksilver* coach overturned, breaking railings and stonework and being itself dragged some distance further along the road. All the outside passengers were thrown off. One, jammed between the coach and the railings, suffered serious injuries, having both of his jaws and four ribs broken. Five other passengers were badly hurt, including the coachman who was "picked up saturated with blood". This was probably the worst coaching accident within the town but the flow of travellers continued, as it does to this day. Brighton continues to be a place of entertainment and pleasure, although many of the 'pleasures' of our ancestors would be totally unacceptable activities today.

Plate 37

The Jolly Tanners, Staplefield, well known in coaching days for its rabbit pies and the cherry trees overhanging the road.

Plate 38

Preston Gate c.1850, the last gate to be passed before the coaches reached Brighton.

Plate 39

The Old Ship on the Brighton seafront was an important terminus for some of the London to Brighton coaches.

Plate 40

The Old Ship, still flourishing today, but with a rather different, and enlarged area between it and the sea.

Plate 41

The carriage road from Castle Square, Brighton, looking towards the southern end of the Pavillion. The Blue Coach Office can just be seen in the distance to the left of the picture.

Plate 42

By the General Coach Office, Brighton; the main point of arrival and departure for coaches. This view is towards the junction between North Street and East Street.

Chapter 10

New Roads for the 'Golden Age'

Until the last 40 years of the coaching era, the years that became known as the Golden Age of coaching and ended with the coming of the railways, coach roads had almost entirely been the upgraded versions of former ancient roads and tracks. For a while these were able to cater for the increasing traffic but the demand was ever for better roads and faster speeds. The old accepted pace of four and a half miles per hour, with lengthy stops for refreshment, was no longer accepted at all. Fast and efficient coaches, carrying their load of impatient passengers to Brighton, needed fast and efficient roads. It was no longer necessary for a coach to call at every small town and village, as sufficient passengers could be found in London and Brighton alone. Roads could be built across the open countryside in as direct a line as possible towards their destination. The cause and the result was exactly the same as that which, 170 years later, was to see the building of modern motorways to ease the burden on other roads and speed the passage of traffic over longer distances. Then, as now, the pre-existing roads continued to be improved, but totally new roads were also constructed.

The two most important new roads between London and Brighton were the one through Merstham, opened in 1808, and from there through what is now Redhill to Povey Cross in 1816; and the road that was opened in 1813 from Handcross to Pyecombe through Hickstead. In terms of interest these are the least rewarding to explore of all the Brighton roads. The reason is that pre-existing settlements were avoided and that, on this most direct route, new road building has continued to the present day. New versions of the A23 keep blotting out parts of the old coach road. The even faster new route, the M23, is simply the latest alternative created by an ongoing process of change.

The 'Golden Age' sections of the road are well documented. J. G. Bishop describes famous rides and drives, and Harper describes the new lengths of roads themselves in some detail, but these new sections of the road have been changed more than any of the others, and the landscape along it has rather less to tell the modern observer than was the case on the other routes. However, even here, there are still many signs that the coaches once came this way and, despite the modern traffic, an investigation of the 'new' roads can still reveal items of coaching interest. It is, however, disappointing as well, since so much that Harper was able to see one hundred years ago has now gone forever.

Smitham Bottom is a long valley with gentle chalk hills rising on each side of it, which provides an easy route southwards through the Downs from Croydon. The northern end of this valley was followed out of Croydon by the Lewes road but, as we have seen, that ancient road climbed out of the valley and on to the drier land of Riddlesdown. The valley bottom was damp and subject to occasional floods. Up to the start of the nineteenth century it was followed by roads which were little more than tracks and only of local importance. Smitham Bottom was, however, of importance for another form of transport as it was followed throughout its length by the Croydon, Godstone and Merstham Iron Railway, which eventually terminated at the great chalk pit and lime works at Merstham. Remnants of the railway are seen at a number of points beside the line of the new road which was built here, including the terrace way crossing the Rotary Field at Purley, and at the bottom of Dean Lane just past Hooley, where the upper part of a small bridge spanning the Iron Railway can be seen.

The advantages of building a new road on the easy gradients between Purley Oaks and Reigate were obvious to coach proprietors and the turnpike trusts. The north–south aligned valley of Smitham Bottom provides easy gradients, and provided the most direct route south to Brighton once road construction techniques improved and it became a practical proposition. Such a road was first suggested as early as 1796 but was strongly opposed by the Reigate and Sutton Trust, who feared loss of tolls. They eventually withdrew their opposition upon payment of £200 a year compensation, and the road opened in 1808.

Purley did not exist as a settlement of any size until the coming of the railways. The small hamlet that stood there was known as

Foxley Hatch. There is a picture of Foxley Hatch held by Croydon library. It shows a very rural scene indeed, with only a few houses near the toll gate where a man on a horse is paying his toll. A woman and child walk down the road past two goats; two donkeys are peacefully ensconced on the grass verge. It was clearly quite a lonely spot, as was the whole of Smitham Bottom. The toll house had a sloping roof on each side, and contained only a living room and a bedroom. The subjects of tolls charged were typical of such a rural area and included droves of cows and horses and flocks of sheep. Like some of the other gates on this busy road, it was a 'night gate', which meant that the gatekeeper had to be available to open it at all hours, a duty usually shared with his wife in daylight hours. Keeping a gate under these circumstances, even on a relatively busy road, was not without its dangers as a report in the *Times* for 19th March 1818 illustrates:

> "Thursday night a daring attempt was made to rob the Turnpike gate house of Fox-le-Hatch, which is situate between two extensive woods on the road to Reigate from Croydon. The villains who made the attempt called in the first instance to the Turnpikeman to open the gate; it was then about one o'clock, but fortunately, as was customary with him during the night, he had left the gate open, and for that reason took no notice of their calling. They attempted to force an entrance at the door and window; the keeper told them he would shoot the first person who entered; they still however, persisted, threatening if he did not let them in they would enter by force and murder him. The gate keeper's assistant then ran upstairs and presenting a blunderbuss at them out of the window, they made a precipitate retreat."

The "extensive woods" each side of the gate would easily have concealed wrongdoers, and made this lonely place particularly vulnerable. Malefactors should have been in little doubt as to what would be their fate if caught. Two gibbets stood between Croydon and Foxley Hatch and there was a strong tradition of punishment for misdeeds in the area. On 30th August 1749 James Cooper, a highwayman convicted of murder and robbery, was executed in Smitham Bottom and then hanged there in chains.

For centuries the only building of significance in Smitham Bottom was the Red Lion beside Lion Green, in what is now the main built-up area of Coulsdon, but was then a remote part of Coulsdon parish. Sad to relate, the Red Lion has recently been demolished. The inn is said to have been built by a highwayman named Alexander, using the proceeds of robbery along this lonely stretch of road. He subsequently continued his iniquitous career by robbing guests at the inn and murdering them if they resisted. Alexander was eventually brought to justice after he tried to rob a young man who was one of two men on a stage coach. While the victim struggled with his assailant the other passenger, an older man named Michael Foster, drove off in the coach to another inn from which he brought back some labourers who overpowered Alexander. The stories have probably been well embroidered over the years but it is quite likely that money from highway robbery contributed to the Red Lion's fortunes. The number of gibbets in the area must have been there for good reason. The recently demolished inn was not the original building, but earlier versions had stood on the same site since 1680. Lion Green, now built over, had another gibbet nearby, the third one in Smitham Bottom. The Green was a famous site for cricket matches, one being played there as early as 1731. It was also a site for prize fighting. On 9th June 1788 a fight took place there between Jackson and Fewterel. The Prince of Wales and many other noble gentlemen were among the spectators, and the prince presented Jackson with a banknote as a reward for his victory. Jackson, later known as Gentleman Jackson, became champion of England. He was a favourite with young sportsmen amongst the nobility and became, in later years, the keeper of the Cock in Sutton.

Smitham Bottom was also known as Hooley Lane, and the Hooley Lane gate stood near the present entrance to Cane Hill at the southern end of Lion Green. On its last day before being finally removed, this gate was the scene of an incident which has become well known in the locality. On that day a nine-year-old boy drove a wagon of wheat through the gate for a local farmer. The wooden-legged toll keeper told the boy that he would be leaving at four o'clock and so after that time there would no longer be any toll to pay. The boy therefore happily spent the money he had been given for the toll, but when he came back he found the gatekeeper still on duty after all. Knowing the lame man would be unable to chase after him he whipped up his horse to race the wagon through the gate. The response of the gatekeeper was to throw the toll gate lamp at him and it fell into the wagon. When the boy's family attempted to return it the following day, the gatekeeper had gone. The lamp remained in the family for many years and is now kept in Purley library.

The 1808 road from Hooley gate to the next gate at Merstham replaced a previous route through winding, muddy lanes. These tracks were important through many centuries for more than local traffic. They served as a route through which the products of important quarries in the Reigate area could be carried north to London. Reigate stone was important for building and quarried at Reigate, Merstham, Gatton and Chaldon. Fuller's earth came from Nutfield and silver sand from Reigate. This traffic was added to at Merstham by greystone building lime from the great chalk pit at Merstham. The old tracks north of Merstham lay off the present road to the west. Parts of it can be followed on tracks and footpaths today. A small section is now a private road between Marling Glen and Gatton Bottom, and the old road eventually emerges in Quality Street, Merstham, a particularly attractive place, now a cul-de-sac but formerly part of the main High Street. It then goes down School Lane, crosses the new main road and down Linkfield Street to Reigate. Thus, in Merstham village, only the small section of the present main road from the Feathers to School Lane follows the pre-1808 line. The Feathers profited considerably from the increase in traffic and rapidly became a prosperous inn. The original building has now gone, having been rebuilt in 1895, but behind it there are old stable buildings dating from coaching days. The Merstham gate lay across the road from Flint Cottage to the stone wall opposite.

Harper writes, "Beside the descent into Merstham was situated the terminus of the old Iron Railway, in the great excavated hollow of the Greystone lime works, where smoke of their burning ascends day and night." The lime-burners used to refresh themselves at the Hylton Arms, later called the Jolliffe Arms. Jolliffe was the name of the lord of the manor of Merstham when the road was constructed, and his brother was one of the contractors, Jolliffe and Banks. There are, of course, no lime-burners left now and the inn, situated at the bottom of Shepherds Hill, has the sad air of a building that has only just managed to survive after its original reason for existence has gone. The great hollow of the lime works is still there however, occupied by the M23, the M25 and the railway. The modern A23, on the line of the 1808 coach road, crosses it on an embankment and the remnants of Merstham's industrial past lie hidden in the trees which conceal piles of chalk waste and occasional remnants of walls which belonged to buildings long forgotten.

There are two different types of milestones on this road, and examples of both are passed before reaching Merstham. Two are of sandstone, one on the east side of the road in Coulsdon soon after the Old Lodge Lane junction; the other by the railway bridge near Coulsdon South station. The miles from Westminster Bridge are given in Roman numerals and those to Brighton in Arabic. The other series continue all the way to Povey Cross. They are of cast iron, triangular in cross-section and with the name of the parish in which they are sited on top. Miles are to and from Westminster Bridge and Brighton. The first of this series lies just to the south of Hooley.

The 1808 road swung right at Gatton Point, south of Merstham, and joined the main turnpike road at Reigate. It cut off a corner of Gatton Park here, and the wall built to establish the new park boundary is mostly still standing. There seem to have been an excessive number of toll gates in this area, but not all would have been in use at the same time. One stood at Gatton Point while another was at the northern end of Wray Common.

The Sutton and Reigate Turnpike Trust had lost revenue as fewer coaches now passed through Sutton, but the new road from Gatton Point still brought customers to Reigate. This was only for a short time, however, because in 1816 another new road was opened to take the turnpike due south from Gatton Point to Povey Cross. An absolutely straight road passes south and over the sandstone ridge, before which is now the town of Redhill but then was all open country. The former site of Frenches Gate is now marked by Frenches Road at the northern approaches to the town. At the top of the ridge south of Redhill a cutting has been made to reduce the height, and another straight road crosses Earlswood Common, a switchback through lovely country with distant views in places. Coaches had now left the drier sandstone soils. The land of Earlswood Common was notoriously damp and provided a serious obstacle to road building before 1816. Road building became a possibility at this time not only because of improved techniques, but also because of the fortuitous discovery of a limestone outcrop in the area which provided a local supply of appropriate construction material. The series of metal milestones continues down this road.

The River Mole is crossed at Salfords Bridge where the road now stands up high above the river level. South of the bridge, the position of a toll gate is indicated by the road name Tollgate Avenue. This was the last toll gate to be removed from any of the roads to Brighton. It was closed at midnight on October 31st 1881 to the accompaniment of cheers from the local populace.

The Chequers is situated where the road to the centre of Horley forks left from the direct Brighton road. It was an important stop for coaches, being halfway between London and Brighton. Parts of the building are original and, until recently, a massive tree trunk remained, all that was left of the ancient oaks that used to stand in front of the building. Just before the Chequers is reached, a small brick building which was once the old forge is situated on the right, which no doubt was a good place for business in coaching days. The coach road then continued on the line of the present A23 and, after crossing the River Mole once more, joined the Classic route at Povey Cross.

For a few years, before 1826, there was a toll gate situated before the junction with Church Road. The last of the cast iron milestones stands south of the road before Povey Cross. Half-buried in the verge opposite the ancient St. Bartholemew's church, it shows 25 miles from Westminster Bridge and 26 miles to Brighton.

The building of new roads on a straight line between London and Brighton had, of course, one prime objective: to make the journey faster on a better road, covering fewer miles. Considerations of speed provide a recurring theme in the story of the Brighton road, and many were the records for individual riders and for coach drivers set both on the Classic route and on the later roads. Some of these records were the result of individual enterprise by sporting young Corinthians in fast curricles. However, it was a great advantage for commercial coaches to achieve fast times and so claim the custom of businessmen operating between London and the coast. The very names of the coaches themselves – the *Quicksilver*, the *Dart*, the *Alert* and the *Comet* – were all designed to emphasise their speed.

In 1813 a Mr Whitchurch caused great excitement by providing a coach which would travel from Brighton to London and return on the same day. Such an idea had never been considered before, but Whitchurch soon had a rival, the *Eclipse*, which did the journey from the Red Office in Castle Square to London and back in six hours. Such a fast journey was almost impossible for passengers to comprehend and newspaper reports of such journeys may initially have been met with some scepticism.

The tone of a newspaper report on the *Eclipse* clearly regarded the following as a report on an astonishing fact:

> "A person, after breakfasting in Brighton, may go to London, transact business, and take his dinner, after which, he may, if he pleases, return to this place to supper!"

In 1816 a group of coach proprietors attempted to cash in on the desire for a fast service by advertising that their coach would do the journey to Brighton in six hours or repay passengers the cost of their fares. It must have been something of a hair-raising experience to ride on this coach as the horses were made to gallop the entire way. On one journey the coachman broke three whips and in one week 15 horses died. Despite the speed the coach never overturned and the service continued for three months until information was laid against the driver for furious driving and the venture ended.

There had always been a tendency for some drivers to race each other and this practice increased, although it was against the law. Fast driving was little to the taste of cautious travellers, and became still less so after a number of serious accidents, for example the race north of Brighton near Preston where the *Dart* and the *Phoenix* were racing each other and a number of passengers were seriously injured. The coachmen were prosecuted. Those who wished to avoid such hazards were wise to buy their tickets from the Blue Office which advertised that "the proprietors will not allow racing, or like folly, with their coaches".

The earliest report of fast times on the Brighton road is of no less a person than the Prince of Wales himself. On the 25th July 1784 he rode from Brighton to London and back via Cuckfield in ten hours; four and a half hours out and one hour longer back. In August of the same year he drove a phaeton with three horses tandem, starting from Carlton House at 1am and arriving at the Pavilion in Brighton just four and a half hours later. With such an example before them it is not surprising that many other riders and drivers responded to the challenge.

The riding record was broken in May 1809 by Cornet Webster of the Light Dragoons, who had a wager of 200 to 300 guineas with Sir B. Graham that he would ride to Brighton within three and a half hours, a speed which must have seemed virtually impossible. Riding one of the blood horses normally used in his phaeton, he completed the trip in three hours 20 minutes. His only stop was a brief one at Reigate for a glass or two of wine. He made the horse swallow what remained in the bottle!

A new record for a coach was set on June 19th 1831 by the *Red Rover*, driven by Philip 'Tim' Carter. He drove from the Elephant and Castle to Brighton carrying a copy of William IV's speech on his first opening of Parliament. No doubt there was haste to deliver the speech but the record also became a splendid advertisement for the *Red Rover* itself, which was then a newly established coach. Carter arrived at Brighton at 8.21 that evening having accomplished the journey in four hours 21 minutes. The feat was even more remarkable because the coach did not run light, as other potential record-breakers were wont to do, but carried 14 passengers on the trip. In June 1832 the same coach did the journey from Brighton to London in four hours ten minutes. The *Red Rover*'s record from London did not last long, however. It was broken by the *Criterion* coach, driven by Charles Harbour, on February 4th 1834, once again carrying a speech by the king. The exceptional speed of three hours 40 minutes was never equalled.

No account of coaching records on the Brighton road can be concluded without mention of the famous drive by James Selby to Brighton and back on July 4th 1888. Selby was a well-known whip and had been driving the road for the previous ten years. The record drive was the result of a wager between some gentlemen of £1,000 to £500 that he would not complete the return journey within eight hours. The coach was a famous one, the *Old Times*, and the drive was to start from the White Horse Cellars, Piccadilly, turning round at the Old Ship in Brighton and returning to Piccadilly.

Selby drove with a party of six. The weather was fine and the horses were changed 16 times during the journey. They started on the stroke of ten in the morning. First change, after only 28 minutes, was at the Horse and Groom, Streatham and took just 47 seconds. Most changes took a little over a minute, but two minutes were spent at Merstham to grease the plates and there was a short delay for the level crossing gates at Crawley. The turn-round at the Ship inn took scarcely a second and the outward trip had taken three hours 56 minutes.

On the homeward run a stop of two and a half minutes allowed the company to descend and stretch their legs for the first time. The plate was greased again at Friars Oak and they continued at a fast pace, taking the corner at Gatton Point at the Gallop. With changes of 50 seconds at Purley Bottom and 55 seconds at Streatham, and further spurred on by the cheers of others on the road, the *Old Times* came to a halt in Piccadilly exactly seven hours and 50 minutes after starting out. It had covered a distance of 108 miles at an average speed, including stops, of thirteen and a half miles per hour. Fortunately Selby had fine weather for his drive and the road was in better condition than it would have been 50 years earlier. However, in those early days the coach would not have been held up at a level crossing! Sadly, James Selby did not long enjoy the fame that the achievement of his great drive brought him, but died, aged only 44, later in the same year.

Not all was speed on the Brighton road, however. Most of the traffic was local, with farmers' carts and drays carrying goods to market while herds of cattle and flocks of sheep were driven along the road and grazed the wide verges while passing. It says something about the width and quality of turnpike roads in the later days of coaching that record runs were not interfered with by having to negotiate such traffic, and nor was speed the main desire of many of the coach travellers themselves. Speed was dangerous in a coach, and those who could afford to wait a few hours could look forward to more sedate journeys. Apart from buying his ticket from the safety-minded Blue Office, the cautious passenger could book a ride in a coach specifically designed with safety in mind. Bishop describes one, the *Bellerophan*, driven by that grand old coachmen, William Hine: "This vehicle was a huge concern, with two inside compartments, carrying four and six respectively, and with ample accommodation for outsides." Such a coach, and its other slow compatriots, did not have a long career on the road, however. Fast journeys had many advantages. They were helped by better roads and better coach design which made the fast journeys safer. However, before too long, even the fastest coach became an anachronism for travel between major towns, being totally superseded by the railways.

Writers who record coaching's Golden Age make much of the roads and the inns, the speed and the glamour. Harper is the only one with a word to say about the animal that underpinned it all: the coach horse. The old roads might have been poor and the pulling hard, but they ensured a gentle pace of travel and lengthy stops where the horses, as well as the coachman and his passengers, could be rested and refreshed. Under these circumstances the same horses could be used for many stages and over a period of many years. Once the age of good roads and short, fast stages had arrived, the life of a coach horse was much harder and the best coach proprietors found it necessary to renew their horses every three years. Chaplin, the greatest coach owner of them all, changed a third of his horses every year.

The cost of horses was, in fact, the greatest extra cost of all in the years when coaching reached its zenith. Huge numbers had to be kept. On the fast routes such as the Brighton road the total number was roughly one horse for every mile covered. The horses were required to pull between ten to twelve miles in a day. Ideally this would be a six or seven mile outward stage and, later, the same distance back, as this meant that they spent the night in their home stable. Some proprietors, however, preferred to let the team do all their miles in just one long stretch each day.

A new coach horse cost an average of £30, but horses could often be bought for less if the previous owner had found them vicious and unmanageable. Such horses were soon made to behave when in the hands of an experienced coachman and harnessed with three other well-disciplined horses. Even cheaper horses could be found; those of doubtful provenance, purchased from shady individuals with no questions asked. An unscrupulous proprietor could turn a blind eye to the possible origins of his new purchase, but it is said that such horses were often run only on night stages!

A good coachman, like a good teacher, did not need to use harsh measures to control his charges, but some individuals made use of a vicious whip, rather like a cat-o'-nine-tails, which was generally known as a 'Short Tommy'. This nasty instrument gave its user control of a horse by what was little short of torture, and its use was strongly forbidden by all the best coach owners.

After their three years were up the coach horses still had many useful years of life ahead of them. Such well-trained horses were readily sold to farmers and to tradesmen who had no need for the punishing pace required of a coach horse. The horses thus lived out their lives in relative ease, perhaps at the plough or between the shafts of a local tradesman's dogcart. They may still have worked hard but were now allowed to proceed at a reasonable pace rather than at 11 miles an hour and, when not working, would have spent their days comfortably grazing, perhaps objects of envy to their successors slaving past in the shafts of a high-speed coach.

In 1813 the route to Brighton was made even more direct by the construction of a new road south from Handcross. The road crossed some of the wettest clay in Sussex, but road engineers were now able to cope with this, even in the notoriously wet Vale of Newtimber where, at last, an easier gradient onto the Downs could be exploited and the ascent of Clayton Hill avoided.

The Bill to allow construction of the new road had been placed before Parliament in 1808, but its passage had not been without opposition. A meeting was held at the Talbot in Cuckfield which resolved that a new road was quite unnecessary. The present road was acknowledged to be the best 54 miles in the kingdom and the time taken to travel to and from Brighton seldom exceeded seven hours. The people of Hurstpierpoint protested that the new road would be an invitation to London cutthroats and pickpockets to invade the area. As with many present-day protests against new developments, the true fears of local people were not entirely those expressed in the report from the local meeting. The protests were, of course, motivated by fears of loss of trade if coach traffic abandoned Cuckfield. In fact, after the new road had been built, the loss was not found to be too great as many of the stage coaches continued to use the Cuckfield road and so take advantage of the services that Cuckfield offered. However Daniel Dench, the respected innkeeper of the King's Head in Cuckfield, removed to the Castle Inn at Hickstead because so many of his fashionable customers were now using the new route.

One other reason for coaches to continue using the Cuckfield road may have been because, according to Harper, the route was:

> "... singularly rural and lovely, and particularly beautiful in the way of copses and wooded hollows, where streamlets trickle away to join the River Adur."

The 1813 road, now mostly on the line of the A23, seems specifically designed to ensure that the traveller ignores any singular beauty through which he may pass. Cars roar down the dual carriageway; getting there is everything and the countryside is an irrelevance. There is, however, lovely countryside still existing nearby, and the pedestrian who deviates from the road will soon discover those wooded hollows where, in spring, bluebells carpet the ground as of yore.

This road, like the modern motorway carving through the fields, was from its inception concerned only with a fast through passage. The modern map shows a typical situation at Bolney. The coach road lies just to the east of the village and the A23 lies to the east again; parallel roads, each in turn moving over into the countryside in the quest for more speed. The Queen's Head at Bolney was a coaching inn, as was the Bolney Stage, a building with some fine old beams and priest holes up the chimney. Bolney toll gate was south of the village, opposite the southern end of the mill pond. As with Warninglid, the site is buried beneath the modern road. No villages are on the coach road. Slaugham, Bolney, Twineham and Hurstpierpoint are all found just off it, and Albourne is in just the same relationship to the coach road and modern road as is Bolney. The villages have all survived as much pleasanter places than they would have become had the road cut through their centres.

The first toll gate on this road was east of Warninglid, where a large roundabout and modern road interchange has now obliterated all trace of the past. A former turnpike road from Staplefield joins here. This is now a lovely rural country lane with great trees beside the road and songbirds abundant. The contrast with the noise of traffic on the main road could scarcely be greater.

The Castle Inn at Hickstead was an important coaching stop, and was also used as a toll house, as, for a while, was a cottage south of the Twineham turning. Unfortunately, although it was a very well-known coach stop, the inn has nothing preserved of interest from coaching days. At Sayers Common, the modern A23 again bypasses the coach road in a repeat of the Bolney situation. The Duke of York was a coaching inn and its former stables are now a cottage behind the inn. The coach road continues through Albourne Street and, further down the route, at the crossroads with the B2117, was Muddleswood gate, yet another site to have disappeared with subsequent road development.

Beyond Muddleswood, where it eventually triumphed over the clay of the Vale of Newtimber, the road took the easiest way up the scarp of the Downs: Pyecombe Hill. Another short section of road was built to link this to the Henfield–Dyke Road route so that the coaches that had formerly climbed up beside the Devil's Dyke could also benefit from the easier way. A new toll gate, Dale Gate, was erected where the two roads met.

Another new turnpike road was also built. This was designed to carry traffic from Cuckfield up the Pyecombe ascent of the Downs to avoid Clayton Hill. The road left the Classic Route at Ansty and passed south through Goddards Green and Hurstpierpoint. There were toll gates near Chalkers Lane north of Hurstpierpoint and at the southern end near Muddleswood. However, this road never became important for London to Brighton coaches. It was turnpiked in 1835 and, in less than a decade, the coming of the railways made redundant any new coaching routes to Brighton.

The road up Pyecombe Hill has been much altered over the years and occupies a wide swathe of cutting into the hillside. Its past appearance can be seen in a fine print by James Pollard. The print shows a coach being pulled at a trot down the hill by a team of four fine chestnut horses. Two young gentlemen sit on the coachman's seat; one in charge of the reins. Two liveried servants sit behind. The closed window must have made the coach stuffy for any inside passenger, but would have kept out the white dust rising from the road. A Dalmatian dog runs in the road beside his master's coach – certainly not a circumstance that would be possible on the modern road! The print is also of interest because it shows how all the hillsides are open sheep pasture, unfenced even on the edge of the road. Beside the road at the bottom of the hill the print shows working limekilns and a great chalk cliff where the hillside is being quarried away. Even today there is a chalk pit at the bottom of the hill, but the chalk face is far back from the road as quarrying has eaten its way back into the slope as the years have passed.

Even though Pyecombe Hill was a new road and on an easier gradient than many that climbed the Downs, it was not without its recorded accidents. In July 1813, not long after the road had been opened, Lord C. Somerset was driving a coach and four down the hill. Unfortunately the leaders' rein broke and the team ran off. It happened that there was a butcher's cart at the bottom of the hill with a fat calf in it. The pole of the coach broke through the tailboard of this cart and went straight into the calf, which was killed. This checked the runaways and none of the horses were hurt.

At Pyecombe the new road joined the Classic route from Clayton Hill, and continued on that route to Brighton.

Plate 43

The first of the iron milestones which mark the new road of 1808, from Gatton Point through Redhill down to Povey Cross on the northern edge of Gatwick Airport.

Plate 44

A four-in-hand on Pycombe Hill. This road provided an easier route up to the South Downs than Clayton Hill on the classic route, but could only be constructed once road making techniques had improved, allowing access across the wet clay lands at the foot of the hill.

Plate 45

Looking down Pyecombe Hill today. The gradient is much reduced to a deep cutting. The chalk quarry at the foot of the hill has been cut back about a quarter of a mile into the hillside.

Chapter 11

The Alternative Routes and the End of the Coaching Age

Apart from the major roads already described, there were two other significant alternative ways to go for parts of the journey to Brighton. One left the Classic route at Horley and returned to it at Cuckfield, having passed through Worth and Balcome. It was turnpiked in 1809. The other left the Lewes road at Newchapel. It served Turners Hill, Lindfield and Ditchling before going over the Downs to Brighton. Coach services between London and Brighton commenced on this road in 1794. The map shows both these roads as quite direct routes but, because they went through fairly small places with only limited numbers of potential customers, they never attained the status of their better-known rivals. Nevertheless they were established coach roads and, being less major, there is no contemporary account of a journey to Brighton that made use of them. The stories of these roads, like those of the Lewes road, were to be discovered along the way, from the landscape, the buildings that remain and the people who live there today.

The country these roads follow is an area of low sandy hills, covered with woods and dissected by many streams. It is a pretty countryside with flowery verges beside the roads and pretty woodlands carpeted with flowers in spring.

Horley to Cuckfield

Coaches on the Classic route which stopped at the Chequers near Horley would usually continue on their way to Povey Cross and Crawley; however the road south through Horley was a good alternative. There was a toll gate here which stood just south of what is now the junction with Victoria Road. It is shown on the tithe map of 1848 completely surrounded by fields. Horley itself was of only very local significance, the old village centre lying to the west of the Brighton road. The town expanded greatly in later Victorian times. This expansion did not impress Charles Harper who, in 1892, wrote:

> "It is situated on an extensive flat, reeking like a sponge with the waters of the Mole, but, although so entirely undesirable a place, is under exploitation for building purposes. A stranger first arriving at Horley late at night, and seeing its long lines of lighted streets radiating in several directions, would think he had come to a town; but morning would show him that the long perspectives of gas-lamps do not necessarily mean houses to correspond. Evidently those responsible for the lamps expect a coming expansion of Horley; but that expectation is not very likely to be realised."

The present inhabitants of the pleasant small town of Horley should be pleased that their town's development, and its important position in relation to Gatwick Airport, has proved Harper completely wrong.

Coach passengers who stopped at Horley could refresh themselves at the Six Bells public house, but to do so had to turn aside to the old village. The Six Bells was a respectable inn in the Golden Age of coaching but less so in former years, when this isolated establishment was one of the haunts of that same Jerry Abershaw who ended his days on the gibbet at Kennington.

South from Horley, along Balcome Road, the old coach road passes through fairly open country, but there is a constricted feeling about it today as it lies between the M23 on one side and Gatwick Airport on the other. For the coaches it would have been quite different as the present airport was then the wide expanse of Lowfield Heath. There was a toll gate at Riceman's Green, just south of the Steers Lane junction, which has, like the Horley gate, left no trace, but the surroundings are still fairly rural although the urban sprawl of Crawley is not far away and soon stretches across to smother the old road. One place that does still stand, however, and must have served many coaches, is a blacksmith's shop situated to the east of the road just south of the Worth Road junction. A stone set in the wall is inscribed with the date 1827. Wrought iron work is still done on the premises today. Apart from this the road has nothing to show of coaching interest until it emerges from the buildings and reaches the edge of Worth Forest. This is part of the huge forested tract which also included St. Leonard's Forest to the east of Horsham, Tilgate Forest and other woodland areas to the east of Worth.

Before entering Worth Forest, the road crosses a westerly flowing stream, one of the most southerly headwaters of the River Mole. The forest still comprises a large expanse of woodland with fine, mature beech and oak trees. Fortunately for coach travellers the forest was a good distance from major urban areas and so does not seem to have been a particular haunt of highwaymen. The forest road climbs over Whitely Hill and then down, out from amongst the trees, to the Cowdray Arms. This inn, formerly the Norfolk Arms, stood beside a toll gate of the same name. From here it gently rises and falls, past Balcombe and across many streams, all of which are now flowing east to join the river Ouse. The main channel itself lies about 30 feet below the raised road surface and this whole section must have been frequently flooded before the embankment was built. Indeed, the whole stretch of road south of Worth Forest is dissected by streams in every valley, and numerous ponds lie behind the hedges and the roadside trees. Apart from the lack of local custom the main reason why this road never became an important route to Brighton could well be because those coaches which were fortunate enough to avoid flood waters could still become bogged down in the ever-present mire.

The last toll gate on this road was at Whiteman's Green, just before Cuckfield is reached. The toll house here survived until recent years but has now been demolished and only the sign for Tollgate Lane marks the site.

Turners Hill to Brighton

The road from Newchapel to Brighton is probably the prettiest of all the Brighton roads. The hilly nature of the country, with its patches of woodland and fields, reveals lovely vistas, and the small towns of Lindfield and Ditchling have preserved an old world charm wherein a coach and four would not look out of place even in the present age. The first London to Brighton coach service to follow this route started in 1794, from the George and the Blue Boar in Holborn to the White Lion and the Golden Cross in

Brighton, but the road never became a major highway, being an old road derived from small country lanes of mainly local significance. Only small towns and villages were situated along it, and it was not as fast as the more direct routes between the metropolis and the coast.

The least interesting part of this road is at the northern end after it turns west from the Lewes road at Newchapel. This is a typical turnpike road with broad verges, now largely overgrown with trees. Near the very start, before the junction with Bones Lane, is the site of the Frogit Heath toll gate. The toll house, which stood to the north of the road, has vanished but a few of the plants from its garden still survive amongst the roadside scrub. Two miles further down the road another toll gate was situated near Perry Farm. This gate and cottage have also gone, but a nearby row of cottages is called Tollgate Cottages.

After the road turns south, it runs by Effingham Park and Crawley Down. The latter was one of the well-known venues for prize fights in coaching days, one famous contest being between Randall and Martin, the 'Master of the Rolls', who later kept the Crown inn in Croydon. South of Crawley Down, a toll gate used to stand at the road junction with Wallace Lane. This road is all along relatively high country following a dry way along the watershed between the basins of the rivers Mole and Medway. At one distinct high point is the village of Turners Hill, where the route is crossed by a road linking East Grinstead to Handcross. The village is an important local centre, looking across the countryside from its ridge. Two village greens remain, as they did in coaching days, with old inns looking across them.

Selsfield Common lies to the south of Turners Hill; a nice little green area with rough grass and trees. This is a shady place in summer and was probably more open in the past when roadside grazing had a practical purpose. There is plenty more shade as the road continues, where it is overhung by fine oaks and beeches, particularly in the vicinity of Wakehurst Place. The Ardingly toll gate was at Hapstead Green on the northern edge of the village. The road continues south, across the Ouse and into the attractive small town of Lindfield.

Many fine old buildings, from coaching times or before, remain in Lindfield. One, Church House, was formerly the Tiger Inn. The Red Lion was a stop for coaches, and three famous coaches, the *Comet*, the *Age* and the *Times*, all stopped there. Two toll gates stood in the town; one on a side road and the other lower down the hill where a cottage which still stands at Number 56 High Street was used as the toll house. Both gates were finally removed on November 1st 1884, and were burnt on November 5th. As with all destruction of gates, there was, no doubt, much joy amongst the assembled populace. Many ponds are passed along this road, but the most lovely of all must be that at Lindfield where the road winds past it out of the town. The size of this pond must have been remarkable, even in coaching days when ponds were so necessary by the roadside. It has clearly been lovingly maintained as a feature and amenity for the people of Lindfield. Sadly, elsewhere, many old ponds have been completely silted up or are so badly overgrown now that they have no economic, as opposed to aesthetic, function.

Just as the Horley to Cuckfield road passed through forest for much of its length, so the road south of Lindfield traversed great tracts of heathland. The first part is now subsumed beneath the urban sprawl of Haywards Heath which, in coaching days, was truly heathland mixed with fields, a remote and rural spot. Some patches of this heathland still remain and become more extensive as the road progresses south.

Soon after leaving Haywards Heath there was a triangular area of common with a toll gate at its southern end – Wivelsfield gate. Then followed more areas of common, most of which are now fields, before the next toll gate at the northern end of Ditchling Common by the Royal Oak public house.

The Royal Oak is a fine old beamed building which served coaches in past days, although it was not a staging post. Sadly, when last seen, it had been closed and boarded up. It is a shame that such an historic inn cannot be kept alive. It achieved a certain notoriety on 26th May 1734 as the scene of a violent attack on the landlord by Jacob Harris, a Jewish pedlar of smuggled goods. The story of what happened is on display in the Royal Oak and comprises one of the more dramatic episodes in the coach road's history. The landlord, Richard Miles, unwisely revealed to Harris that he had taken a considerable sum of money, about £20, that day. Harris determined to rob him and attacked him, slashing his neck twice. Seeing a serving maid watching, he stabbed her too and then ran upstairs and stabbed the landlord's wife who was ill in bed and had called out to ask what was going on. He ransacked the inn but found nothing of value, then fled north.

He eventually reached the Cat Inn at West Hoathly and sought safety there but found it full of smugglers who told him the militia were out hunting for someone who had done two murders at the Royal Oak. It appears that the landlord at the Royal Oak had not immediately died of his wounds but had managed to get out to the road and raise the alarm. Harris realised that the landlady at the Cat was looking at the blood on his sleeves, so he fled to Selsfield House and took refuge there on a ledge in the parlour chimney. This hiding place served to conceal him from the riding officers who came to seek him there, but it was not a good refuge for long. The officers decided to stop at the house to dry out their wet uniforms. They lit the fire below the chimney where Harris was hiding and, overcome by the smoke, Harris fell down into the flames, landing right at the feet of the very people who were seeking him. He was arrested and was identified by Richard Miles before the latter died of his wounds.

Harris was hanged in Horsham but his body was left on a gibbet at the north end of Ditchling Common where it remained for many years. This gibbet became known as 'Jacob's Post'. It was said to be haunted, and also to have the power to cure many illnesses. Pieces were broken off and kept as charms by local people. A replica post stands on the site today, but a small remnant of the old post was displayed in the bar of the Royal Oak.

The toll gate at the north of Ditchling Common was retained until the start of the twentieth century, not for the collection of tolls but to prevent cattle straying from the common. It was removed after a motorcyclist was killed, having crashed into it. The common itself is a wonderful open space of heathland dotted with trees, across which the road gently rises and falls. Little has changed here since coaches and carriages were the main vehicles on the road. It is just the same type of country that the coaches crossing Haywards Heath and St. John's Common would have seen; a piece of eighteenth century scenery that has survived into the twenty-first.

North of Ditchling village is a very typical turnpike road with its wide verges, ditches and oaks in the hedgerows. The little town itself is very attractive, with old buildings and an interesting museum which, amongst other coaching antiquities, houses the old milestone from distant Povey Cross. There were two toll gates in the town: one at the north end, the toll board of which is in the museum, and one at the south end where a building sticks out to the edge of the road. It may have been at one of these toll gates where a disappointing stag hunt started in March 1827:

> "On Wednesday morning a stag was again turned out before the Brighton Harriers, at the Turnpike Gate, on the Ditchling Road. The field was a good deal disappointed, as the stag could not be urged to run. It is the last that was purchased. After trotting at a pace which any person might have kept up with him, he was taken on the roof of a stable not far from the place where he was turned out."

This was the same unfortunate animal that declined to provide sport at Bramber a week later, and finished its days on the spit as solace for the disappointed huntsmen.

The Bull in Ditchling was a regular stage for the London to Brighton coach on this route. Fresh horses were particularly necessary here before climbing the hill to Ditchling Beacon. In October 1806, at another Ditchling inn, the White Hart, the landlord was woken at 4am by a noise and, on investigating, disturbed two men, one of whom drew a pistol. The landlord tackled him and caught him by the hair while the other escaped. The landlord found he had caught a notorious smuggler and murderer named Robert Bignall. Both men had escaped from Rochester gaol, and Bignall's accomplice was later apprehended by the landlord of the Swan at Chailey. Bignall was eventually hanged, with the execution witnessed by a crowd of three thousand people.

The road up Ditchling Hill was ingeniously engineered to aid the passage of coaches. It wound up the hill in a series of bends to ease the gradient and it also ascended, as did a number of the roads up the Downs, by a series of gigantic steps to reduce the pull for horses at intervals on the way up and to ensure the coach should not slip too far back if it should start to do so. Some of these steps have survived to the present day, although they have now been smoothed out. The few near the top are the best preserved.

The wide views from the top of the hill are as impressive as those from above Clayton and Beeding. Some dew ponds remain near the road, made, as elsewhere, to hold water for sheep on the dry downland pastures. Cows and arable fields are now more plentiful here than sheep, except on the steeper slopes. It is still a lovely place, with wide, open skies. Modern car drivers speed along this pleasant road, in greater comfort than the coach passengers, but without hearing the song of the skylarks which still sounds overhead. Gradually the road slopes gently down to Brighton.

Ditchling Hill was much less used after a new road was made to link Ditchling with Clayton Hill in 1830. It must have been this road that was followed by the coach after an accident which occurred in December 1838:

> "On Saturday afternoon, as Mr. Cussell, the driver of the Brighton *Globe* Coach, was in the act of getting upon his box at Ditchling, eight miles from Brighton, the horses suddenly started, and threw Mr. Cussell under the wheels, which passed over his body. He survived the accident only about a quarter of an hour. The horses, being free from control, started off at the top of their speed, without a driver. There were four inside, and only one female outside, who had the presence of mind to keep her seat, and refrain from screaming; and it is worthy of remark that the horses continued their career for a mile and a half, passing through a Turnpike-gate, before they were stopped by some labourers in going up Clayton Hill."

The End of the Coaching Era

Although the mass of modern traffic was undreamed of, in the heyday of coaching all the different roads to Brighton must have seemed, to the people of that age, to be teeming with vehicles. By 1835 the Golden Age of coaching was at its zenith. In *Roads and Vehicles* Anthony Bird gives impressive figures for the whole country. Seven hundred mail coaches and 3,300 stage coaches were running regularly. Thirty-five thousand men were coachmen, guards or horsekeepers. A hundred and fifty thousand horses were actively employed pulling coaches. Fodder for the horses was one of the most important products of agriculture, and the coaching trade sustained thousands of inns. J. G. Bishop tells us that in 1822 there were 62 coaches running daily between Brighton and other places, of which 39 served London.

By the end of the Golden Age coaches were as perfect as it was then possible for them to be; well built and well maintained; well driven and safe. The finest coach of all was probably the *Age*, Stephenson's old coach, owned in its later years by Thomas Ward Capps. It was always splendidly horsed and Bishop tells us of Thomas Capps:

> "Nothing but the best satisfied him. All the fittings (and even the colouring) of 'The Age' were unique: the pole chains, etc. were of burnished steel. The 'ribbons' too, were of the daintiest – Paliser's best make – exciting the envy and admiration of the coaching fraternity. And then the horse cloths! Who ever saw their match, edged as they were with broad silver lace, and adorned with gold mountings, and having at each corner (embroidered in coloured silk and silver) the Royal Crown and a sprig of laurel? Altogether, though there were many other splendid contemporary coaches, 'The Age' may be regarded as the best representative of coaching in all its glory. Singularly enough, in later days, it represented it in its decline, being the last coach on the road!"

It seems only right that the *Age* was the last regular coach on the Brighton road, not finally being removed until 1862. The *Age*'s horse cloths and other coaching memorabilia were, according to Bishop, presented by Mr Capps to Brighton museum in 1887. Sadly, on enquiry, the museum could find no trace of them.

On the main roads, such as those between Brighton and London, the coaching age ended with bewildering suddenness. In 1838 an Act of Parliament authorised the carrying of the mails by rail. The London, Brighton and South Coast Railway opened on September 21st 1841. Part of this line was roughly parallel to the turnpike roads of the Croydon and Reigate Trust. In the 1820s, an average of 36 coaches a day used this road. By 1845 this number had decreased to only two. So little money was taken in tolls that, in 1850, the trustees stated, "the toll income has decreased so considerably that the repair of the road has ceased". The same was equally true on other roads. As early as 1836 a special meeting of the trustees of the Horsham and Steyning Turnpike resolved to oppose the railway from London to Brighton on the grounds that it would result in a reduction of tolls, making it "doubtful whether the future receipt of tolls will realize a sufficient sum to maintain the said road and pay the interest of debt owing to the shareholders". After the railway started operation the trust struggled on with a steadily diminishing income and, in 1885, decided to demolish the toll house on the new road to Old Shoreham and sell the site.

Those coach owners who had sufficient foresight and who had the means to do so took their coaches off the road and joined the new railway companies. These prescient individuals included William Chaplin, the greatest coach proprietor of them all, who joined the board of the London and Birmingham Railway. Coachmen made all the money they could and then sold their horses and destroyed their coaches. Their problem was a simple one: the railways were cheaper and faster, and only those rich enough to possess their own carriages could afford *not* to travel by rail. As Bird says, "despite initial dislike and fear of the railways few people were going to pay 6d a mile or more to travel at ten miles an hour in a stage coach when they could travel three times as fast for a third of the cost and have greater comfort and safety into the bargain".

As the railways rolled remorselessly into Brighton, so the places that had served the coaches lost their relevance. Castle Square was no longer the terminus for travel to and from Brighton and the coach offices which stood in that vicinity soon served their last customers. The Blue Office, at the corner of North Street, was pulled down in October 1845 and the last coach to leave The Red Office was the *Victoria* on the 8th of the following month. The last coach to run on the Lewes road was on July 12th 1846; just one month after the railway had arrived at Lewes.

Of course, the end of the mail and the stage did not mean the end of coaching. It was not until the next century that the motor car replaced private carriages. These continued in use on all roads, for then, as now, the railways did not go everywhere. Turnpike roads remained in operation and still charged tolls for the coaches that used them, but without the regular custom of public services, they gave little profit to the trustees. The *Times*, on October 31st 1865, announced:

> "The whole of the remainder of the Gates and Bars on the south side of the Thames (61 in number),

will be Abolished tonight at 12 o'clock – so that, as provided for in the Act of Parliament and from the 1st November, 1865, the roads shall be free of tolls."

The toll gates had always been much disliked, as with any system of taxation, and their abolition was an occasion for rejoicing. Sometimes, as we have seen, they provided material for public bonfires in the streets. Not all can have been removed immediately however, as the Salfords Gate, the last to be kept open on the Brighton roads, was not removed until 31st October 1881.

The users of the toll-free roads were now almost entirely private individuals. One by one the regular coach services were discontinued. When a coach was sold the horses were sold with it, and it is recorded that so many horses were being sold, and so many coach companies had gone out of business, that a fine coach horse might fetch a price of only ten guineas when, a few years previously, it could have been sold for ten times that amount.

Without coaches to drive, the coachmen too lost their jobs and, with them, their key position in society. J. G. Bishop provides a list naming many who were famous coachmen in their day: Bob Pointer, Black Sam, Crossweller, Captain Gwynne, the Hines, Charley Lee, Sheel, Harry Holdsworth and many more. He records with sadness those who were once household names, at least in the places through which they drove to Brighton, but were now gone and hardly even memories.

Bishop also reproduces an extract from a 'local journal' which eloquently laments the passing of the coaches:

> "Alas! that ever the day should come when Castle-square should be cadless and coachless – when the stroke of twelve noon should not be the signal for every soul who can see beauties in a perfect four-in-hand to transfer himself to its vicinity – when its ample space should no longer be filled with half-blood teams, covered with rich trappings, prancing and curvetting and showing their rounded limbs and glossy skins in the sun – when the far-reaching whip should cease to be flourished aloft in triumph or cracked in the full exuberant spirit of the road!

> Alas! that the day should come when four-in-hands should be reckoned amongst the things of the past, and take their place with the broad-wheeled wains of our ancestors – 'The Age' and 'The Times' should not be the fastest-going things on the road, and be as much outstripped in the race of time as the laziest carrier's cart that ever crawled along the surface of the earth!
>
> "Yet all this is come to pass, and we are not old men. We have seen Castle-square a mere desert at twelve o'clock; we have beheld it stripped of that mighty corps of coachmen, porters, cads, and others, that long exercised in it the sway of power; we have turned the corner of the Blue without having the breath squeezed out of our body; we have passed the narrow straits of the Red without having our corns trodden upon; we have doubled the Spread Eagle without breaking our shins over heaps of luggage. Nay, more – we have not heard one jest, nor seen one practical joke played off. Nor smiled at one sally of humour or exhibition of character in that most fertile of all places for jests, comicalities, and practical jokes – all has been 'dull, flat, and unprofitable.'
>
> "Thus and therefore is it that, in bidding farewell to the stage, we do it with all kindness and no little sorrow."

Not all, however, would concur with this misty-eyed recollection. In the *Kilkenny Moderator* of March 13th 1852, the following appeared, entitled *The good old coaching times*:

> "We all of us remember the misery of a journey on a coach 10 or 15 years ago. Who the people were who used to write and talk about the pleasure of sitting behind 'four spanking tits,' we never could understand. The tits (horses) never spanked when we were perched behind them on the black shelf which was called a seat, and was about as comfortable as a mantelpiece. Then again 'the box'

was considered a great thing to secure. We never intrigued, or fee'd, or struggled for it. It entailed an uncomfortable position, with the trouble of holding a bunch of hard leathern reins in your hands while the driver got down; and the bore of listening to his commonplace uninteresting conversation, when he kept his place. If you went behind you had no room for your legs, as they hung dangling over the wheels. If it was cold you were frozen; if it rained you were soaked; and if it was dusty you were smothered. All was as bad and dreary and miserable as it well could be. Thank goodness, however, at last the coaches have gone; and all the coachmen, and guards, and loaders, and hostlers, and helpers, and hangers-on-generally, with them. The coarse hurried dear inn-dinner is gone; the troublesome passengers who go down to drink brandy and water at every stage, and would talk to you afterwards, are gone; the horses, whose histories you were supposed to be interested in – how the leader had been picked up for a 'fippun' note, or the wheeler had worked ten years in the Brighton *Highcharger* – are gone, and in their place we have the civil unpaid guards, the rapid exhilarating transit, and all but actually reasoning steam engine of the glorious railroad."

Whether memory recalled the glory of coaching days or the misery of coach travel, one group of people were soon quite forgotten. The old coachmen must have stood in bewilderment as their world collapsed around them, leaving them bereft of livelihood and of purpose in life. One can only imagine the thoughts of those former lords of the road as they stood outside a coaching inn and watched the steam train roaring by. A poignant quotation is printed by Selway:

"'A coachman,' said one in 1852, 'if he really be one, is fit for nothing else. The hand which has from boyhood grasped the reins, cannot close upon the chisel or the shuttle. He cannot sink into a book keeper for his fingers could as soon handle a lancet as a pen. His bread is gone when his stable door is shut.'"

Some coachmen ended their days in poverty, but many found work connected in some way with horses; the more fortunate in the service of gentlemen who had come to know them through frequent travel or had even been taught by them to handle a coach. Many became innkeepers, for example Ambrose Pickett who had driven the *Union* and the *Item* from Brighton. He became the landlord in North Street, Brighton, of the appropriately named Coach and Horses. Probably the very last door through which a memory of Brighton's golden coaching age could be glimpsed closed in June 1893. In that month died Philip 'Tim' Carter, driver of the *Red Rover* in the record-breaking run of 1831, and one of the very last of the old coachmen to pass away, surely to find a friendly inn awaiting him and a fine team of fresh horses ready in the stable.

The coachmen may have gone but a surprising amount of the roads they knew and the inns they stopped at still remain. This is particularly surprising on the Brighton road, with its constant evolutionary change. Some of the inns today still seem to be awaiting the jingle of harness which heralded the arrival of a coach and the bustle of activity its arrival called forth. On some of the roads, particularly on the more remote downland tracks, it does not strain the imagination to see the passage of ghostly horses steaming into the air as they pull up the dusty chalk slopes.

Certainly the "glorious railroad" was vastly superior and more comfortable than the coaches could ever be. In modern times, the motor car, which often unknowingly follows the old turnpike routes, is faster, and is certainly more convenient than the coaches ever were. Yet the coaching age, short as it was, will always have its own special place in history, and it was at its finest on the Brighton road.

Plate 46

The Royal Oak, north of Ditchling Common. A useful halt for coaches on this relatively minor road, and the scene of a gruesome murder that lived long in local legend.

Plate 47

The construction of the Clayton railway tunnel. The coming of the railway marked the end of commercial coaches on the Brighton roads. The obstacle of the South Downs was penetrated and transport between London and the sea entered a new age.

Bibliography

Abdy, Charles. *A History of Ewell.* (1992)
Ackroyd, Peter. *Thames: Sacred River.* (2007)
Albery, William. *A Millennium of Facts in the History of Horsham and Sussex. 947–1947.* (1947)
Alderman, Henry Martin. *The History of Brighton and Environs.* (1871)
Alderton, Mary. *Bourne Society Local History Records.* Vol.XI (1972)
Armstrong, J. R. *A History of Sussex.* (1961)
Auction particulars for the manor of Caterham. Surrey Record Office 3883 Folder 5 of 19.
Austen, Brian and Upton, John. 'East Sussex Milestones – A Survey', *Sussex Industrial History*, Winter 1972–73 and 1976.
Bannerman, Ronald. *Forgotten Croydon.* (1933)
Barton, Alan. *Passenger Transport in Surrey.* Surrey Archaeological Collections 78.
Batley, James. *The Godstone Gap.* Local History Records. Vol.XIV 1975
Baylis, D. A. 'Retracing the first Public Railway', *Living History Local Guide.* No.4.
Bird, Anthony. *Roads and Vehicles* (1969)
Bishop, John G. *A Peep into the Past. Brighton in the Olden times.* (1880)
Blew, William C. A. *Brighton and its Coaches. A History of the London and Brighton Road.* (1894)
Bloom, J. Harvey. *Bygone Streatham.* (1926)
Box, A. Ed. *Old Taverns of Surrey.* Surrey Archaeological Collections IXX
Broadbent, Una and Latham, Ronald (Ed.) *Coulsdon Downland Village.* (1976)
Brown, O. S. Buss, Brian. Davis, Bernard. *The Chequers, a place in Horley's history.* (1997)

Cary's Roads (1817)
Cary's Survey of the High Roads from London (etc.) (1810)
'Catalogue of Materials and Fittings of the Toll House situated at Sutton Lane', Surrey Record Office. 65/5/122–123.
Chapman, Brigid. *East Sussex Inns.* (1988)
Chapman, Brigid. *West Sussex Inns.* (1988)
Cheal, Henry. *The Story of Shoreham.* (1921)
Chouler, W. H. Horley. *Pageant of a Wealden Parish.* (1975)
Christie, M. E. et al. *Ditchling* (1937)
Cooper, W. V. *History of the Parish of Cuckfield.* (1912)
Copeland, John. *Roads and their Traffic. 1750–1850.* (1968)
Crofts, J. Packhorse, *Wagon and Post.* (1967)
Danehill Parish Historical Society Magazine. Vol.4, No.4. 1991.
de Candole, Henry. *The Story of Henfield* (1976)
Edwards, J. *A Companion from London to Brighthelmstone, in Sussex.* (1801)
Erredge, J. A. *History of Brighthelmstone.* (1862)
Farrant, Sue. 'The Development of Coaching Services from London to Brighton, c. 1750–1822'. *Sussex Genealogist and Local Historian.* Vol.7, Nos.3 and 4. March 1986
Fuller, G. Joan. 'The Development of Roads in the Surrey–Sussex Weald and Coastlands between 1780 and 1900'. *Transactions of the Institute of British Geographers* 19. (1953)
Gilbert, E. W. *Brighton, Old Ocean's Bauble.* (1953)
Gower, Graham. *A brief history of Streatham.* (1980)
Gower, Graham. *Balham. A brief history.*
Gwynn, Peter. *A History of Crawley.* (1990)
Hall, Helena. *Limpsfield Past and Present.* (1960)
Harper, C. G. *The Brighton Road.* (1892)
Harper, C. G. *Stage Coach and Mail in Days of Yore.* (1903)
Hearne, Sir Gordon. *An itinerary of Streatham.* (1980)
Hills, W. H. *The History of East Grinstead.* (1906)
Hoare, J and Upton, J. *Sussex Industrial Archaeology. A Field Guide.* (1985)
Holmes, Frank. *In and around old Horsham with Frank Holmes.* (1987)
Home, Gordon. *Epsom. Its History and its surroundings.* (1901)

Hooper, Wilfred. *Reigate: Its Story through the Ages.* (1945)
Jackson, Alan A. (Ed.) *Dorking, a Surrey Market Town through twenty centuries.* (1991)
Jowatt, Evelyn M. *A History of Merton and Morden.* (1951)
Kehler, Margaret K. (Ed.) *Memories of Old Dorking.* (1977)
King, Maud Egerton, *Round about a Brighton Coach Office* (undated)
Lane, Elizabeth. *Early days in Horley, Sidlow and Salfords.* (1958)
Lucas, P. G. 'Local Carriers in the 19th Century.' *Danehill Parish Historical Society Magazine* Vol.4, No.4 (1991)
Maggs, K. 'Croydon Local Environmental Information Service, 2. Milestones and Tollhouses.'
Margary, Ivan d. 'The Development of Turnpike Roads in Sussex.' *Sussex Notes and Queries.* Vol. XIII, No.3. (1950)
Marshall, Charles J. *A History of the old village of Cheam and Sutton.* (1936)
Martin, Alderman Henry. *The History of Brighton and Environs.* (1871)
Melville, Lewis. *Brighton: Its History, its Follies, and its Fashions.* (1909)
Mogg, Edward. *A survey of the High Roads of England and Wales.* Vol.1. (1816)
Mogg, Edward. *Patterson's Roads.* (1829)
Mountfield, David. *The Coaching Age.* (1976)
O'Shea, E. W. 'Ashcombe Round House.' *Sussex Industrial History.* No.13. 1983.
Onslow, the Earl of. *The Road in Surrey.* Surrey Archaeological Collections. XLVI. (1928)
Packham, Roger. 'Famous Inns of Surrey – The Red Lion, Smithan Bottom'. Reprinting, Hampton Hamilton (F. H. Le Queux) from *The Surrey Magazine*, March 1900.
Ransom, P. J. G. *The Archaeology of the Transport Revolution. 1750–1850.* (1984)
Rawlings, D. S. 'The Roads and Tracks round Danehill'. *Danehill Parish Historical Society Magazine* Vol.4, No.4 (1991)
Resker, Rev. Robert E. *The History and Development of Purley.* (1916)

Searle, Mark. *Turnpikes and Toll-Bars.* (1930)
Selway, N. C. *The Regency Road. The Coaching Prints of James Pollard.* (1957)
Sheppard, Ronald. *Micklam. The Story of a Parish.* (1991)
Skuse, Peter R. *A History of Whyteleafe.*
Smail, Henfrey. *The Worthing Road and its coaches.* (1943)
'Smith's Actual Survey of the Roads from London to Brighthelmstone.' (1800)
Smith, Robert P. *A History of Sutton. A.D. 675–1960.* (1957)
Sowan, Paul W. 'The Croydon Merstham and Godstone Iron Railway. A short chapter in a Long story.' *Local History Records* Vol.l45 (2006)
Tharby, W. C. 'The Croydon and Reigate Road.' *Local History Records.* IV. (1965)
'The Round House, Ashcombe.' *Sussex Archaeological Newsletter.* 41. (1983)
Tristram, W. Outram. *Coaching Days and Coaching Ways.* (1893)
'Turnpike Trusts.' East Sussex Record Office. County Reports. No. 3. Sussex. (1852)
Vale, E. *Mail Coach Men.* (1967)
Vardey, Edwina. *History of Leatherhead. A Town at the Crossroads.* (1988)
Wigstead, Henry and Rowlandson, Thomas. *An excursion to Brighthelmstone made in the year 1789.* (1790)
Willis, Cloudsley S. *A short history of Ewell and Nonsuch.* (1931)
Wilson, Violet A. *The Coaching Era.* (1922)
Windrum, Anthony. *Horsham, An Historical Survey.* (1978)
Wright, Maisie. *A Chronical of Cuckfield.* (1991)

Sources of Illustrations

The author is particularly grateful to the Archives and Libraries who provided the illustrations used in this book, and gave permission to use them:

Royal Pavilion and Museum, Brighton and Hove
Plates: 39 'The Old Ship Hotel' FATMP 000400
41 'The Carriage Road from Castle Square to St. James' Street' c. 1834, producer I. Bruce FA 207913
42 'By the General Coach Office, Brighton' by Robert Dighton 1803 FA 014001
47 'The Construction of the Clayton Tunnel' FA 102179

Croydon Library
Plate: 10 'High Street, Croydon, looking North' c. 1830 by J. Henry Drage, after C. Hawkins 143.4 High Street

CTG Publishing.Com
Plates: 34 'Stage Coach' by Dubourg after James Pollard
44 'Four in Hand' by J. Gleadah after James Pollard

Dorking Museum
Plate: 23 'The Bull's Head, Dorking'

East Grinstead Museum
Plate: 15 'East Grinstead Toll Gate' Photograph 1864

London Metropolitan Archives
Plates: 3 'The Cock Inn at Sutton' by James Pollard p7495950
6 'The Brighton Coach outside the Bull and Mouth, Piccadilly' by E.F. Lambert p752137x
7 'View of the Elephant and Castle Inn' by James Pollard p5398504
9 'Kennington Turnpike Gate' 1865 Photograph SC/GL/PHO/B/LI/KEN M00 23286CL

Reigate Priory Museum
Plate: 32 'The Old Tollhouse, Reigate Hill' Watercolour, unsigned

Sutton Library
Plates: 8 'Kennington 1842' from contemporary newspaper engravings in 'Turnpikes and Toll Bars' Mark Searle
21 'Morden Gate' (as above)
30 'The Cock at Sutton' painted by Thomas Rowlandson
38 'Preston Gate' c. 1850

West Sussex County Library Service
Plates: 26 'The Venture Coach at Henfield' PP/WSL/PC004407
27 'The Chequer Inn Yard, Steyning' PP/STJSM/1983.55.11.5.1
28 'Toll Gate, Bramber' PP/STJSM/1993.116
35 'Old Toll Cottage, High Street, Crawley' PP/WSL/PC003109

All present day photographs by the author.

Every effort has been made to trace copyright holders and to obtain their permission for the use of copyright material. The author and publisher apologise for any errors or omissions in the above list, and would be grateful if notified of any corrections that should be incorporated in future reprints or editions of this book.

Acknowledgements

A book such as this is inevitably an amalgam of many small parts. Items of information from local history societies and from individuals with special knowledge of their own locality are a vital addition to the mass of information held by record offices and libraries.

Members of societies whose information has been particularly helpful include Brian Austen, Sussex Industrial Archaeology Society; James Clube, Leatherhead and District Local History Society; Brian Phillips, Federation of Sussex Local History Societies and P. G. Lucas, Danehill Historical Society. I am most grateful also for correspondence from John Brown, Streatham; Bernard Davis, Crawley; Geoffrey Mead, Brighton; E. N. Montague, Sutton; Pat Wood, East Grinstead and John D. Matthews, Purley. There are many others whose names I do not know who have shown interest and have given help with what I have been doing. In particular I am grateful to the many innkeepers who have told me about the history of their hostelries including stories of specific incidents, and have shown me relics of the coaching age which remain in the buildings and contents of the inns.

Much important information, particularly in regard to maps of the roads, was provided by the Record Offices of West and East Sussex and of Surrey. The British Museum Department of Prints and Drawings was helpful with locating illustrations and with information about them. Local museums were unfailingly obliging and often held unusual and interesting artefacts as well as historical references and possible illustrations. The most notable of these were the museums of Brighton, Ditchling, Dorking, Cuckfield, East Grinstead and Steyning.

Lewes Library had some references to be found nowhere else, as did the Minet Library in Lambeth and the Guildhall Library.

Further useful information came from the libraries of Croydon, Guildford, Sutton and Worthing. To all these I am extremely grateful, as I am also to the numerous other libraries in the towns along the old coach roads. In all of them, the staff were both knowledgeable and helpful.

In the exciting hunt for illustrations of the coaching age a number of establishments were particularly helpful and welcoming. Kate Shawcross and Valery Murphy, at Sutton Central Library, provided me with some really excellent pictures of coaching times. The libraries of Croydon, Reigate, Morden and East Grinstead all held pictures of interest, showing their towns as they were when coaches followed the important routes through them. The Metropolitan Archives were a treasure trove of pictures pertaining to the roads at the London end, and the Worthing Library picture archive was the best and most useful online source of pictures I discovered. In Brighton, Jenny Lund and Karen Wraith at the Brighton Museum and Art Gallery went to endless trouble seeking out pictures of Brighton and its coaches, some of the most fascinating pictures of all.

Last, but not least, to my son Peter, whose help with putting together the digital images has been invaluable, and to my wife, Elizabeth, for her consistent help and support.

About the Author

Geoffrey Hewlett studied Geography at the University of Southampton, and was Head of Geography at Whitgift School in Croydon. He is particularly interested in the evolution of the landscape, from the combined standpoints of geology, landforms, vegetation and human activity. From an early age he was encouraged by a family, steeped in natural history, to look with curiosity at everything around him and try to understand how and why the landscape he walked through had evolved.

Long residing in the South East of England, he has a deep love of the countryside encompassed by the Downs and the Weald. On walks through this varied landscape he frequently encountered the old roads to Brighton and became increasingly interested in uncovering their history.